READY SET GROW!

10 Success Strategies for Winning in the Workplace

Veronica J. Holcomb

ADVANTAGE WORLD PRESS

Published by Advantage World Press
P.O. Box 452
South Orange, NJ 07079
www.advantageworldpress.com

Publisher's Cataloging in Publication Data

Holcomb, Veronica J.
Ready, Set, Grow! : 10 Success Strategies for Winning in the Workplace
Veronica Holcomb. — 1st ed.
South Orange, NJ, Advantage World Press, 2005.
p. ; cm.
Includes index.

ISBN: 1-932450-77-7

1. Success in business. 2. Interpersonal relations. 3. Industrial relations.
4. Office politics. 5. Employee motivation. I. Title.
HF5386 .H65 2005
650.1— dc22 0501

Printed in the United States of America
First Edition: March 2005

SPECIAL SALES

Advantage World Press books are available at special bulk purchase discounts for use in sales promotions, premiums, or for educational purposes. Special editions, including personalized covers, excerpts of existing books, and corporate imprints, can be created in large quantities for special needs.

For more information, write to:
Advantage World Press
Special Markets Department
P.O. Box 452
South Orange NJ 07079

Fax (973) 324-1951
www.advantageworldpress.com
E-mail: specialmarkets@advantageworldpress.com

Other titles by Advantage World Press

Investing Success: How to Conquer 30 Costly Mistakes & Multiply Your Wealth!
By Lynnette Khalfani

Zero Debt: The Ultimate Guide to Financial Freedom
By Lynnette Khalfani

You Can Afford to Retire
By Michael Kresh

Praise for Ready, Set, Grow!

*"*Ready, Set, Grow! *is an excellent resource for a lot of reasons: The book is content rich, comprehensive in addressing all aspects of professional and personal development, and contains exercises that are easy to complete, yet thought provoking.* Ready, Set, Grow! *is also general enough to be used by all those interested in developing themselves as professionals, not just as managers/supervisors. In this book, you'll find insights into the real-life issues professionals grapple with but may not feel comfortable verbalizing – such as initiating small talk in social situations and 'playing the game' in the workplace."*

Elizabeth M. Madison, MA, CRC , Program Director, NADAP, Inc.

*"*Ready, Set, Grow! *is a long-awaited book for adults in, entering, and returning to the work force, and the academic settings. I plan to use it as a reference book and possible textbook in all of the college courses I teach, and adult presentations I do."*

Dr. Maude E. Robinson, Preceptor/Academic Counselor,
St. Joseph's College School of Adult and Professional Education

"Rarely will you find a leadership book with such a targeted message as Ready, Set, Grow! *This book says: 'Get to the top – and stay there!'"*

Rev. Dr. Therman E. Evans, MD, PHD

"Veronica Holcomb changed my life. If you can't hire her as your coach, then reading her book, Ready, Set, Grow! *is the next best thing."*

Harry Carr, CEO, Simpler Networks

"For anyone that wants to get ahead at work – especially women trying to break through the glass ceiling – Ready, Set, Grow! *gives you the formula for success."*

Leslie Ashford, Executive Development Consultant, Aetna Inc.

"Regardless of where you are on the corporate ladder, Ready, Set, Grow! *will help you get to the top. Veronica's easy steps will assist you in identifying your REAL potential, and more importantly, show you how to achieve it."*

Thomas W. Mann, Chief Operating Officer, TRM Corp.

*"*Ready, Set, Grow! *provides a simple yet powerful framework to help you find that elusive balance of success and personal satisfaction in the workplace. These practical ideas are relevant no matter where you are in your career."*

Jeffrey Sugerman, CEO, Inscape Publishing

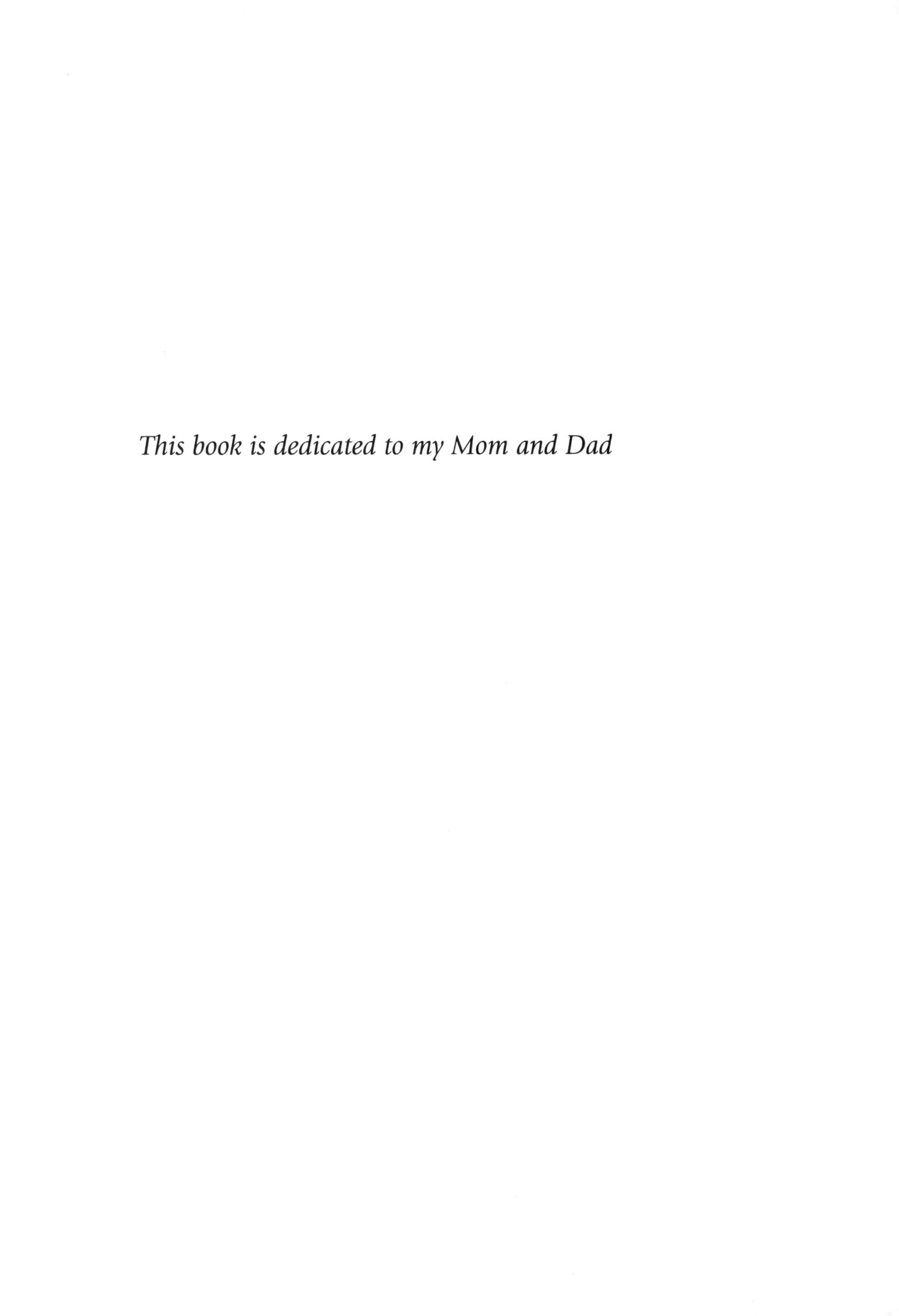

This book is dedicated to my Mom and Dad

Acknowledgments

Many times during the writing of this book, I would compare the process to that of having a baby. From conception to labor and delivery, it's a painful, yet joyful process. But this is what has allowed me to bring to the world all of who I am, and the thousands of people who have allowed me to coach, teach and mentor them are part of it too. This baby looks like us.

There's an old African saying that goes…it takes a whole village to raise a child. I'd like to modify that a bit and say it takes a whole team to write a book. I could never have written this book without the help of some very special people.

First, I'd like to thank Denise Barnwell, my coach, friend and spiritual sister, who inspired (perhaps prodded) me to write this book. Through Denise, I found the confidence to take that first step. Just as young children learning to walk are a little wobbly in the beginning, in the first few months, I was unfocused and fell down a few times. Diane DiResta, an old friend and colleague, was there for me. Cinda Gaskin put my feet on solid ground, gave me solid direction and support, and then worked with me chapter by chapter. Thank you, ladies.

Thank you, Debbie Beaton, for being the priceless gem that you are. Debbie encouraged and supported me as well as catching the double negatives and incorrect use of commas. And I'd like to thank Juanita Bodden, Tawana Bivens Rosenbaum, and Marcia Brown for their help in editing and designing the book.

No one had more patience on this project than George Rodriguez. His good humor and amazing talent produced a beautiful book and made the difficult times easy.

I've run a few short races and know the importance of having people cheering for you during that last mile. Barbara Spilka brought me over the finish line with her incredible insight, experience and remarkable eye. Thank you, Barbara — you made a difference.

I am especially indebted to Tom Pojero for his special insight on Work-Life Balance. He is a top-notch executive and an exceptional father and role model. Thank you, Val Serrano and Lisa Egbono Davis, for your insights as well.

I am appreciative of my friends and family from Christ Church and Morningstar Christian Community Center for your prayers and your belief in me. To all of you whose stories I have told (changing names, of course, to protect the innocent), thank you.

I am grateful to my family: Stacey, Dani, Mom, John, Brenda, Keith, Kyle, KJ and Kevin, for their love, patience, support and encouragement.

Finally, and perhaps most importantly, I'd like to thank my husband, best friend and biggest fan, Richard Holcomb, whose unconditional love and support is all the success I need.

Table of Contents

Foreword

Like a fine gardener meticulously and deliberately cultivates a prized garden to realize its full growth and beauty, Veronica Holcomb, a master coach and mentor, cultivates and grows people. I know because, more than a decade ago, I was one of those seeds waiting to bloom.

I met Veronica during a very difficult period in my life: I was aimless, jobless, and clueless about what to do with my career. I was referred to Veronica by a mutual colleague, who thought Veronica's straight forward, no-nonsense approach was what I needed.

Despite the fact that I was unemployed, and couldn't really afford her rates, she did not treat me any differently than her most senior level clients, who paid thousands of dollars more for her services than she charged me. In her wisdom, she knew that making me pay something for our sessions – whatever I could afford – would cause me to value the process. And through it all, she didn't make me feel embarrassed or beholden, but rather treated me with dignity and respect. Little did either of us know that her sacrifice and intervention would lead me to training and ministering to thousands over the next 15 years through the business and ministry that she coached me to develop, Healing Dialogues.

The title of Veronica Holcomb's book *Ready, Set, Grow!* perfectly describes her coaching approach. She first gets people to a place of *readiness* through a process of self-awareness, feedback and reflection. Then she *sets up* an environment of success by providing tools and exercises for individuals, giving them the confidence and skills crucial for them to *grow*. Her principles outlined in the book will be for the reader as they have been for me: a road map for personal and professional success. You will see yourself in the heartfelt anecdotes, and the tools will prove to be thought provoking and illuminating.

Through the years, Veronica has been the voice of conscience and wisdom for me: a bar setter and trailblazer. Today there are many self-proclaimed coaches. Yet very few rise to the ranks of a "master coach." A master coach is someone who has the ability to make even the most talented leader want to obtain even greater heights and at the same time show him or her the value of humility and gratitude. A master coach makes every moment count and sees the importance of our mistakes as well as our accomplishments. A master coach is not afraid to tell the truth to the most imposing figure and at the same time can rally the faintest of hearts. Such a master coach is Veronica Holcomb. She knows how to make us better human beings — and better human beings make a better world.

Reverend Carol E. Dougherty-Steptoe
President & CEO
The Dialogues Organization
New York, NY

Introduction

In today's climate of rapid technological change, global competition, impatient investors, corporate distrust, and an uncertain economy, greater demands are being placed on leaders, managers and staff to produce results in a way that inspires trust, confidence and admiration.

Few people succeed without exceptional talent or technical expertise; however, personal acceptance skills, as well as the softer skills of leadership style, self-awareness, managing others, persuasion and cooperation, are vital in today's workplace for those who want to maximize job performance and pursue distinct career goals.

The demands of today's workplace require successful participants to hone skills that cause them to stand out above the pack. Savvy individuals will master those skills that allow them to effectively influence, communicate, motivate and develop others.

Intelligence, talent and hard work are not enough to guarantee success. Daniel Goleman, in his book *Emotional Intelligence*, argues that the focus on IQ ignores a crucial range of abilities that are critically important to how we do in life. The secret to success in the workplace is in effectively coupling essential "soft" skills with technical and functional expertise or "hard" skills. Only in this way can individuals work at their highest level of effectiveness and impact.

People are often surprised, frustrated and unprepared when they discover the ability to achieve success in the workplace based on their hard skills is limited. There are untold numbers of highly intelligent professionals who couldn't lead their way out of a paper bag. There are still others whose interpersonal skills are so poor that even with sterling technical skills, they fail in the workplace. Lacking the softer skills of style, manner, relationships, projection and presentation, they engage in negative behaviors such as arrogance, poor listening skills and/or insensitivity to others.

There are many highly talented and bright individuals who enter the workplace feeling less than confident. They may feel intimidated by those they perceive as more intellectually gifted and fail to understand the advantage that soft skills can afford them. They are hesitant to put themselves into situations for fear they would expose what they perceive as their more modest and limited capabilities. As a result, they don't take advantage of opportunities to develop their talents and advance their careers.

The lucky ones are those who have been identified as having potential and are subsequently mentored, coached and nurtured along. Unfortunately, most people have been on their own…until now.

This book is for everyone who wants to succeed in the workplace. Well-honed soft skills will allow you to use your hard skills at a greater level of impact and influence and give you a competitive advantage at work. Personal development is not a sprint. It's a marathon, and it takes planning, proper nutrition, strategy, other people, understanding yourself, understanding your competition, courage and grit. If you want to be successful, *Get Ready, Get Set, and Grow!*

Veronica J. Holcomb
New York, New York
March 1, 2005

How to Use This Book

- The chapters do not have to be read in sequence. With the exception of Chapter 10, Crossing the Finish Line, you can read only those chapters that are of most interest to you or meet a particular need.

- The exercises and activities contained in the various chapters can be worked on alone, with an accountability partner or as part of a group.

- There is no need to speed through the entire book. Take your time and complete each exercise. I'd like you to relax, complete the exercises, and engage in a process of true self-discovery. *Ready, Set, Grow!* is not quite a substitute for having a real-life coach working with you, but it's the next best thing.

Whether you are a civil servant interested in making a major career change to the corporate world, a full-time trainer venturing out as an independent consultant, or an employee simply desiring to improve her networking skills, *Ready, Set, Grow!* will enhance your work experience and give you a competitive edge.

Some people may choose to use this book as required reading or a curriculum outline for new supervisors. Others may use it as a blueprint for training individuals who hold managerial positions in either a nonprofit or a for-profit entity.

However you use *Ready, Set, Grow!*, I encourage you to incorporate its strategies and recommendations into your personal and professional activities. By doing so, you will greatly expand your sphere of influence, your presence within your organization, and your effectiveness on the job.

CHAPTER 1
Workplace Savvy

I love professional baseball. When I'm at the stadium I score the game in my scorebook and simultaneously listen to it on my Walkman. What an incredible difference learning to keep score has made in my ability to understand and enjoy the game. It helps me feel connected and fully engaged in the action.

After so many years of enjoying baseball this way, I simply cannot sit idly in the seats and watch. If the ump makes a controversial call I'm armed with my Walkman, listening to the announcers in the control booth, so that I can savor every fun-filled moment.

In my profession as a Leadership Development coach I have observed people who enjoy or at the very least don't mind "playing the game" in the workplace. These people are as engaged in the action as I am while watching a baseball game. Playing the game at work may not be nearly as much fun as watching the New York Yankees, but it need not be the burdensome and painful task that many people experience. As in watching baseball, what makes the difference is your ability to understand what's going on around you.

Get ready

Work is work. The politics, game playing, backstabbing, secret agendas, dishonesty, egos, and cut-throat behavior can wear you down. And it doesn't matter where you work or the type of organization you work for, e.g., education, business, healthcare, not-for-profit, faith-based, there are *always* politics. Much of your success will depend on how successful you are at negotiating the politics or "playing the game."

I've worked with many people who loathe the idea of "playing the game." Most feel that their work should speak for itself and that the quality of their work should be sufficient to merit advancement and recognition. Sorry. This is one of the myths that continue to permeate our culture despite its extreme distance from reality. It is simply not enough to be good at what you do. You have to do what you do in a way that demonstrates credibility, trust, and integrity. Very few people work alone; most work as part of a team. Hence, your ability to establish and maintain effective relationships is paramount and, at certain levels, your workplace survival depends on it.

People who dislike "playing the game" usually don't understand it. My purpose in this chapter is to debunk some of the myths and negative thinking associated with "playing the game." I also want to provide you with skills to help you win.

I'd like for you to write down seven to ten reasons why you dislike playing the game (see **Success Step 1.1**). Your reasons can be because of behaviors you've seen in yourself or others who actively engage in the game, perhaps from within or outside your organization. After you jot them down on a piece of paper, hold it aside. I'm going to ask you to revisit this later.

Success Step 1.1 | What I Dislike About Playing the Game

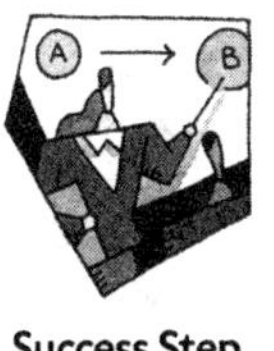

Success Step

1.	
2.	
3.	
4.	
5.	
6.	
7.	
8.	
9.	
10.	

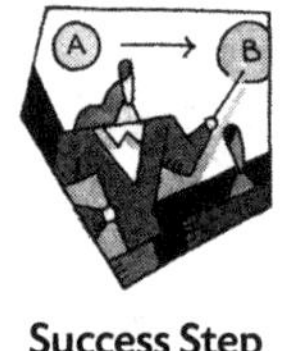

Success Step

Success Step 1.2 | How Savvy Are You at Playing the Game?

Answer the following True/False questions:

1.	I have a mentor.	T | F
2.	I regularly keep key players informed of my project status.	T | F
3.	My peers are among my most valuable resources.	T | F
4.	I have personal allegiance with co-workers at all levels of the organization because I treat them with respect and consideration.	T | F
5.	I am aware of the resources that I can offer.	T | F
6.	I take time to listen to other's requests for assistance even if I can't help them directly.	T | F
7.	I find effective ways to say no without jeopardizing future support.	T | F
8.	I set aside my own agenda and listen to other people's ideas and rationales.	T | F
9.	Before presenting an idea or action plan, I attempt to discover where key persons "stand" and formulate a plan to handle it.	T | F
10.	I demonstrate my commitment to the organization by going the extra mile when necessary.	T | F
11.	I attend social functions and support the organization's values, goals, and mission.	T | F
12.	I demonstrate and maintain a sense of humor.	T | F
13.	I am aware of the political climate, but present myself as apolitical.	T | F
14.	I deal with upper management persuasively.	T | F
15.	I rarely become impatient with the political process or make procedural errors.	T | F
16.	I am rarely too direct and I almost always consider the impact of my words and actions on others.	T | F
17.	I always project the consequences of my actions.	T | F
18.	I am sensitive to how people function and how organizations function.	T | F
19.	I anticipate where the land mines are and plan my approach accordingly.	T | F
20.	I view corporate politics as a necessary part of organizational life and live within that reality.	T | F
21.	I keep abreast of the rumors on the grapevine.	T | F
22.	I do favors for people.	T | F
23.	I volunteer for undesirable assignments or committees.	T | F

24. I know what makes my boss "tick."	T | F
25. I keep an open mind about people. I don't make quick judgments.	T | F
26. I toot my own horn whenever I can.	T | F
27. I have contacts in various parts of the organization.	T | F
28. I try to always look and feel my best.	T | F
29. I make a sincere attempt to be open to other people's perspectives even if I don't agree.	T | F
30. I can develop rapport with many different people.	T | F
31. I am good at establishing common ground with others.	T | F
32. I can usually get others to respond positively to me.	T | F
33. I understand people well.	T | F
34. People feel comfortable and at ease around me.	T | F
35. I can empathize with others.	T | F

Scoring | Give yourself one point for each True answer.

☛ *If you've scored* **30-35**, *then you should mentor others whenever possible.*

☛ *If you've scored* **28-32**, *then cash in your political chits.*

☛ *If you've scored* **27 or less**, *rest assured that you can turn this around with a little effort.*

What are politics?

Politics are the inter-relationships that exist within an organization. They comprise the formal and informal structure of an organization — its written and unwritten rules. Understanding the politics of your company means that you understand where the real power is and how to access it, or at least garner the ability to influence that power. Learning a company's politics can be very complicated and sometimes overwhelming, but when reduced to its most basic definition, it is the ability to connect and interact well with others.

If you have no interest in moving up in your organization or in having greater influence and impact, you don't have to play. You really don't. However, at some levels and in some positions you're going to find yourself on the field whether you want to be there or not.

Why do you have to play?

Doing great work isn't enough. You need people. It's not very likely that you will make things happen as the Lone Ranger in any organization. You need others to rally around you and your ideas. In addition, a widely developed network of supporters and advocates will facilitate the accomplishment of your work. These people see value in supporting you and in being part of your goal attainment. How you achieve that level of support is key.

Is this a personality contest? And if it is, how much control do you really have? Suppose some folks just don't like you? Admittedly, having a warm and friendly personality is a plus, but if you want to increase your influence, you must let people get to know you better. And, like it or not, you'll need a strategy.

Why do we dislike playing the game?

Most people in today's workplaces are aware of the enormous changes that have occurred in recent years with respect to workforce diversity. Thirty years ago, certain jobs were deemed jobs that only men could fill, while others were viewed as jobs exclusively for women. Today, women and men occupy many positions they would not have held a generation ago. As a result, many people feel a great deal of conflict in trying to reconcile the traditional roles they grew up with while playing out their contemporary roles.

> *Recently, I met a woman in her thirties, the mother of three small children. She told me that her mother had chosen not to work outside the home. Instead, she stayed home and took care of her children during their formative years. Her mother attended all of the children's school plays, helped them with their homework, and had dinner on the table when dad arrived home each night at 6:00. Her father's role was to work and pay the bills. Today, this young mother is not doing as her mother did. Rather, she has a demanding full-time job. And the realities of today's fast-paced life do not allow her to fit into the traditional role her mother maintained. But because she has internalized those more traditional values, she feels guilty and frustrated.*

This is not unusual. Many women experience the agony of role conflict that results from having internalized more traditional roles but living and working in a contemporary society. Internal conflict and guilt can surface when women feel they *should* be at home but they're at the office. And when at home, they're on the computer checking e-mail or unconsciously attempting to manage their homes the way they manage an office. (This often causes problems with objecting family members who must remind mom that they are not her employees.)

Workplace behaviors can be aggressive. For some, playing the game is too much of a capitulation and a denial of the behaviors they have grown up with and internalized. The tension, guilt, and frustration of trying to reconcile the internalized perspective with the day-to-day reality leave some people drained, with little energy for thinking about, much less playing, the game.

> *Rory is a former teacher who grew up with four brothers and sisters in a working class family. After leaving teaching, Rory navigated his way into a very responsible and senior role with a major telecommunications company. He never imagined that he'd be making the kind of money that he now makes and that he'd be wielding the influence that he does. Despite his success, Rory doesn't quite "fit in" with the others at his level. He secretly harbors feelings that he doesn't deserve to be there. Playing the game is not something he focuses on.*

The reality is that playing the game can intensify internal conflict that many folks bring into the workplace. It becomes another area that requires focus. And because we don't understand it well, we're confused and unsure of how we really feel about playing the game. Further, when we are already concerned about meeting deadlines, making presentations to senior management, conducting staff performance appraisals, attending PTA meetings, and providing the nightly homework assistance our children need, something has to give.

> *In Rory's case, it was the family. He postponed celebrating his 25th anniversary with his wife to attend a business meeting in Europe. In the case of the young mother, she managed her time at work very carefully by spending little time with others, barely taking lunch breaks, and dashing out of the office promptly at 5:00 pm to get home on time. The result in both cases was guilt, frustration, disappointment, worry, anger, and stress.*

I gotta be me!

Learning to work within a well-established culture that is different than your own is difficult because you cannot help but bring your ethnicity, culture, background, and experiences to the workplace. With that come many preconceived notions of how certain groups should behave. Women with children who work long hours are often criticized for working long hours, unlike their male counterparts. Women who behave in an aggressive way can be off-putting to many people, while men who exhibit a laid back or conciliatory attitude may be seen as weak and ineffectual leaders. The ensuing frustration and confusion leaves potential game players not knowing what to do or how to behave. Imagine being on the baseball field without knowing whether you were playing offense, defense, first base, or the outfield.

The key is to integrate who you are with what is expected of you in the workplace. Recognize what must be done for you to develop relationships that are necessary for your success. You must determine how far you will go, and how much you will give up in order to succeed. Draw a line in the sand in order to protect yourself, your family, and your relationships, and don't cross it. Be yourself and reflect authentic and consistent behaviors — let your words and your music match.

Many people find playing the game to be fraught with pretense, compromise, and a lack of integrity. They also believe that in order to be successful they must give up their identity and hide their true feelings for the sake of a better position. When they find themselves being nice to people they don't really like or when they support projects they don't really believe in, they feel as if they're selling out. When they're invited to social events by co-workers, they feel put-upon unless they believe that the invitation is based on true "friendship." Hence, they make excuses to avoid attending work-related gatherings, retirement dinners, and invitations to have lunch with colleagues. Not smart. Remember: it's not just what you do; it's how well you do with the people with whom you work. Relationships matter. In fact, relationships are the key to your success. Those who are willing to play the game correctly take advantage of opportunities to interact with people and build relationships. You can do this and still be "you."

Your integrity is not at stake because you choose to play the game. In fact, quite the opposite is true. Maintaining your integrity is to your advantage. People who have integrity are people who can be trusted and engender the confidence of others. Violate your integrity and you'll lose your credibility. And once you lose your credibility, you can't get it back. Be relentlessly honest in all situations. Remember, adapting your behavior to fit a particular situation doesn't mean you're compromising your integrity.

Think about it. We adapt our behavior to meet the needs of different situations all the time. When I'm speaking with my four-year-old nephew, my conversation, behavior, and body language are radically different than when I'm speaking with a senior executive. Similarly, I carry myself and speak differently with my daughter than I do when I'm with a friend. Like most people, I wear many hats and fill many roles: mother, wife, daughter, aunt, business partner, friend, and executive. These roles reflect different dimensions of who I am and my ability to adapt to different situations and different people. In order to interact and connect well with others, which is the heart of political game playing, you must adapt your behavior and employ distinct skills for effective communication in different relationships.

When a baseball player can play more than one position, e.g., third base, shortstop, and second base, he's called a utility player. He has great value to the team because he can easily fill in when another player becomes injured or needs a day off. You can become a stronger version of "you" by increasing your utility value to the organization and by becoming more flexible and multidimensional.

Confidence

Lack of self-confidence is a key reason why people don't want to play the game. Self-confidence exists when you believe in yourself and in your abilities. You will not develop experience in playing the game without confidence. Similarly, in order to develop confidence in playing the game effectively, you need experience. So what do you do? Start small. Find an area where you can experience the satisfaction of success without taking much risk. I often recommend that people join the board of directors of a not-for-profit organization. The organization would greatly benefit from your experience and you can develop your game-playing skills in a low-risk situation. Further, your salary is not tied to your performance.

I also tell people seeking experience in playing the game of office politics to find a mentor. This person can help you interpret the politics in your organization and can advise you through this new area in your career development. In addition, enlisting a small group of supporters who are concerned about your growth and development can strengthen your confidence. These supporters can be family, friends, or colleagues who cheer your successes and help you through difficult times. Finally, study others. Read this book and gather other resources that will help you focus on developing your confidence. You can't win the game if you don't play the game. And you won't play well if you lack confidence.

According to Jeff Howard, of J. Howard & Associates, three areas of confidence are important to be successful in the workplace:

Intellectual confidence
You need to believe that you are smart enough to come up with new ideas, learn new things, and understand the complexities of your work environment. More people have more confidence in this area than in the other two areas. In fact, overconfidence in this area causes most people to ignore the next two.

Social confidence
With this kind of confidence, you are comfortable dealing with new people in social settings and interacting with others in ways that are enjoyable to them as well. You don't have to be a social butterfly, but spending an evening hugging the wall or buttonholing one person will not help your cause. One of my clients used to take the opportunity of the social gathering to grab a colleague and discuss business — at length. Eventually, she was given the feedback that it was okay to relax. People genuinely wanted to spend non-work-related time with her and enjoy a friendly conversation. It's a balancing act. You are expected to act professionally (no dancing on tables and swinging from chandeliers please) *and* to connect with people in a relaxed and casual way.

Political confidence
Being politically confident, you understand the big picture, the political relationships, and the written and unwritten rules. In the United States, during presidential elections, large corporations will court the Democrats and the Republicans by giving money to both candidates running for office. No matter who is elected, they will have access to the people in charge based on the connections they have previously made. I am not suggesting that you start handing out bribes or making donations. I am, however, encouraging you to get to know where the power base is in your organization and find a way to gain some influence there.

The three types of confidence are interconnected as shown in **Illustration 1.1**.

Illustration 1.1 | The Three Types of Confidence

Illustration

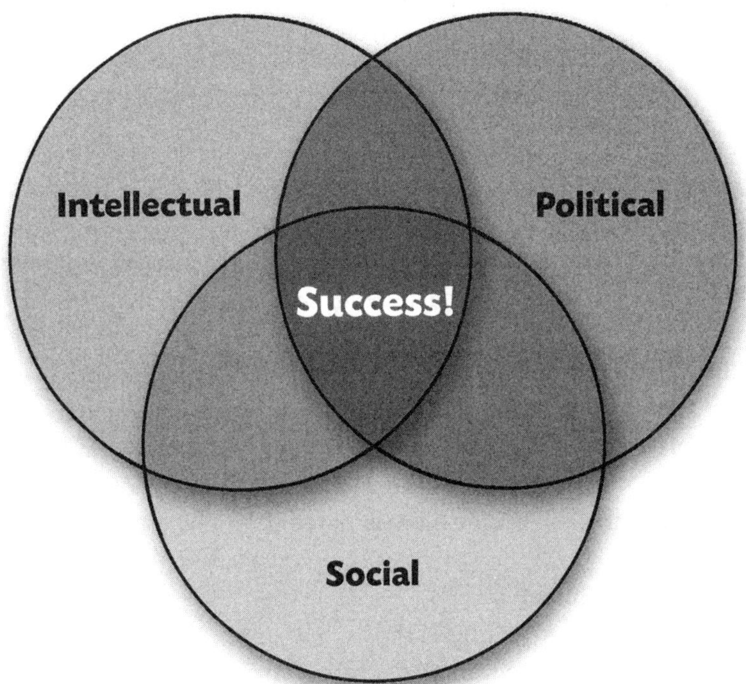

You need political skills to deal effectively in work-related social situations, and intellectual and social skills to gain political influence at work. You need to integrate all three in order to deal with the complexities and challenges of the job in a way that matches the goals of your superiors.

> *Kyle is very good at that. When a new senior manager came on board a few years ago, she stressed return on investment (ROI). Kyle continued to deliver great results, but began couching them in a way that stressed ROI. Recently, another senior manager began stressing Client Effectiveness. Now Kyle is delivering her great results in a way that stresses Client Effectiveness. Kyle is someone who uses her political skills to deliver results in a way that positions her to be noticed by senior management. She uses her intellect to develop strategies that deliver results. Kyle also uses her social skills to inspire her troops and maintain relationships with colleagues and seniors.*

People who struggle in playing the game are often strong in only one area of confidence. Because they've not developed confidence in the other areas, they are limited. I often meet people who have tremendous confidence when it comes to their intellectual skills. They have done well because they are smart and have worked hard. Unfortunately, in the workplace, intellect and hard work are simply not enough.

> *Peter earned both his undergraduate degree and MBA from an Ivy League school. He is very bright, but has poorly developed people skills and little political awareness. As a result, he is chronically unemployed or underemployed. He is totally incompetent when it comes to reading the political tea leaves and writings on the wall. When the ax is about to fall on his head, he hasn't got a clue.*

Don't let this happen to you. The only way you can develop confidence in playing the game is to get out there and play. No one can become a competent or even mediocre ballplayer by sitting in the stands watching the game. Similarly, you'll never become confident in playing the game if you sit in the bleachers or on the sidelines complaining that you're not getting time on the field. You have to make it happen.

How do we get in the game?
The first item of business in getting in the game is to fish in the right pond. Most people underestimate the importance of working in an environment that best suits their style, personality, intellectual pursuits, and talents. But, like a fish out of water, working outside your element for too long will cause you to struggle — emotionally, mentally, and spiritually.

While I'm not a football fan, my husband and many of our friends love the game. So I've made many attempts to get with the program. I've attended games with them. I've had them diagram and explain the game to me countless times. I've tried to develop an emotional connection to a team by taking an interest in individual players and their families. I've even tried to connect with teams based on the color of their uniforms. Nothing has worked. I usually lose interest after the first few weeks of the season. The result has always been the same — I didn't get it. Finally, one day I did. I accepted the fact that I just don't like football. And because I fundamentally don't like it, it's a struggle for me to learn it.

Your ability to understand and play the workplace game is determined by how much you enjoy what you do and how well suited you are to the environment in which you work. If you don't like your job, you should assess what your likes and dislikes are to determine what motivates you in a work environment. It is also important that you understand and evaluate the core mission of your organization to see how your position contributes to these goals. Think about whether your company's mission is congruent with your core values and beliefs. How do the various divisions and departments interact to meet the company's goals and objectives. Do your company's leaders perform their roles with integrity?

Career counselors and career assessment centers offer instruments that can help you do this type of introspection to identify a work environment that fits. We'll look at some behavioral style models in a later chapter. These models will give you a better sense of your personal style and the best work environment for you.

Assuming that you are in the right environment, here are some first steps to getting in the game.

Pressing the flesh

Pressing the flesh is an old political term that describes the process politicians engage in as they go from event to event shaking hands, kissing babies, and doing whatever it takes to connect with people. You certainly don't want to appear to be campaigning in a workplace environment, but it is important to market yourself and to develop a constituency. The more you understand and can read how others like to communicate, make decisions, and receive feedback, the more you can connect with them by delivering your message in a style that satisfies those needs.

To help you understand how to read people's needs, see Chapter 7, *Who's Who in the Workplace Lineup*.

First, it is important to understand *your* particular behavioral style. If you are someone who is active and outgoing, but very task-oriented, you are probably someone who has a need to control things or people. We call this a "Dominance" style. Your style of interacting with people may be very quick, direct and results-oriented. Dominant styles enjoy working in difficult environments and overcoming challenges. People exhibiting this behavioral style at work tend to be very impatient listeners. While this style may work for you with people who are similar, it can turn off the people in your work environment who like to spend more time chatting and getting to know you.

If you're someone who is active, outgoing and more people-oriented, you probably fit the "Influence" behavioral style. You enjoy a friendly, more fun-loving environment. Your style is somewhat gregarious, optimistic, and talkative. You may find yourself getting carried away and perhaps talking too much or monopolizing conversations. Careful, this can also turn some people off.

On the other hand, if you are someone who tends to be somewhat quiet and reserved, but people-oriented, then yours is the "Supportiveness" style. You enjoy an environment where maintaining status quo is the norm, where people cooperate to get things done. You are someone who is cooperative, easygoing, and pleasant. You may be challenged with sudden change or with asserting yourself in situations or conversations so that you can be heard.

If you find that you are quiet and reserved, but more task-oriented or analytical, then yours is the "Conscientiousness" style. These analytical types would prefer to do away with social functions altogether. And, if roped into one, say as little as possible as they anxiously check their watch so that they can make an appropriate exit. Conscientiousness types prefer a reserved and business-like environment.

Who knows you?

There's and old adage that says, "It's not *what* you know but *who* you know that counts." The belief is that the ability to do a good job is not nearly as important as knowing the right people who can and will do something for you. I suspect that some of you know a few people who are mediocre performers but have done pretty well, based on their knowing the "right" people. This does happen, but the results of this approach are limited.

The truth is…it *is* what you know, but it's also *who knows you.* Doing a good job is very important, but it is equally important that people from disparate parts of the organization know you as well. You must develop a broad organizational network of supporters, friends, and people who know your work *and* with whom you have a relationship — even if the contact with them is infrequent.

Invest the time to develop organizational friendships; preferably *before* you need them. Get to know the people you work with, their perspective on things, and what's important to them. In this way, you can effectively communicate and frame their issues and concerns. You can tailor what you say to match or support their goals. And you can provide them with feedback on the issues they are most concerned about.

Take time before or after a meeting to engage in one-on-one conversations with your colleagues on non-work-related topics. This is time well spent. It shows people that you care about them. Ask about their kids, their interests, vacations, or an ailing parent. Invite them to lunch, for drinks after work, or to share a ride to a work-sponsored social event. Your objective is to know people on more than just a work level and to have them get to know you.

As a team player, stay open to ways you can support your peers. Take an interest in their projects and their goals and become a viable resource to others. If you have relevant information that you think would be helpful in supporting them, why not share it? It's very probable that they'll return the favor because you've positioned yourself as a reliable key player. And, if you are promoted at some point and your peers become your subordinates, having positive relationships already established is a win-win situation for everyone.

On occasion, you will work with people who are not trustworthy and do not have your best interests at heart. Like it or not, you have to work with these people too. My advice to you is simple: don't give away the candy store and always, always protect the family jewels. If a situation arises that exposes the untrustworthy person as such, deal with it swiftly and directly.

All of this may seem a little manipulative. Perhaps it is, but it takes work to develop *any* relationship — parent-child, boss-employee, and partner-partner. There's always give and take.

Networking

Let me begin by saying what networking is not. It is not an excuse to hang out by the copy machine and chat for extended periods of time. Nor is it simply exchanging business cards at the local watering hole or identifying people around the organization who can "do something" for you or with whom you enjoy gossiping.

Networking is a reciprocal process of developing and calling contacts for information, advice, career opportunities, business leads, referrals, and moral support. It is asking others for help when you need it and it is giving help to others when they need it. Networking is about *building relationships*.

Developing and maintaining your network means calling people on a regular basis to say, "how are you doing…how are things going?" Some of the best networkers that I know make it a point to have a conversation with a senior person or key stakeholder in their organization at least once or twice a quarter just to talk about what's going on and to seek the senior's perspective on the business.

I can hear the objections from you readers out there, reminding me of how busy you are and what precious little time you have to do your job. I hear you and I understand. But developing a constituency *is* part of your job. It's not in your job description, but the higher you rise, the greater the expectation for you to have internal resources to draw upon for support and with whom you have influence. Be thoughtful and strategic about who should be a part of your network and how often you need to be in contact with them.

On **Success Step 1.3**, Networking Strategy Worksheet, identify the following: In Column I, list people with whom you have regular contact, i.e., daily or weekly. In Column II, identify a second tier of people with whom you have irregular contact, i.e., you see them in occasional meetings. In Column III, identify people with whom you have infrequent contact; you see them at yearly meetings, conferences or workshops.

Success Step

Success Step 1.3 | Networking Strategy Worksheet

I	II	III
Regular Contact	**Irregular Contact**	**Infrequent Contact**

Everyone on the list need not be internal to your organization. For many of you, your list will include outside customers and vendors. Once you identify these contacts, decide how to connect with them and how often. Some connections may simply be an extended conversation in the hallway before or after a meeting. Others may involve social contact outside the office or a mentoring session with them. List these people and be realistic. If you are an entry-level employee, attempting to get time on the CEO's calendar may be an exercise in futility. There needs to be a reasonable connection between you and the people on your list.

Now for the hard part: scheduling the meetings. If you schedule but one or two business lunches a month, that's probably twelve to twenty-four more networking lunches per year than you are currently having. Over a period of just a few years, you can make tremendous progress toward developing and maintaining networking relationships. This favorably positions you for future support when the need arises.

Words fail me

Perhaps the single most important skill in successfully playing the workplace game is communication. What you say, how you say it, when you say it, and to whom you say it goes a long way. A statement with great content but poorly timed delivery can create a negative perception of you in the sight of others. And today, with so much communication taking place through e-mail and conference calls, paying attention to content *and* delivery is all the more important.

Many people say things in e-mail they would never say if they were speaking to you in person. Their tone can be condescending, their attitude can be off-putting, and their actions can be interpreted as cowardly. For example, someone who chooses to deal with a sticky situation through e-mail and then copies their boss is acting in a cowardly manner. Deal with the person directly. If you cannot resolve the issue, then take the matter higher.

There are occasions when you may have to be the bearer of bad news, communicate a rigid new policy, or say things people generally do not want to hear. And, unfortunately, there are times when these messages must be communicated via e-mail. I suggest you start with a positive comment to engage the reader. Then you can diplomatically introduce the problem at hand. E-mail offers a great way to connect with others both personally and formally, but use it wisely.

Small talk, big problem

Most people do not look forward to attending work-related social functions — especially the kind where folks are standing around making conversation with drinks in hand. Many people simply hug the walls or huddle with people they know and with whom they feel comfortable. Moving in and out of various groups of people does require some practice and a few stock opening and closing lines, such as "How is everyone? I don't believe we've met, my name is… What department are you from? Do you live in the area?"

What do you talk about after the connection is made? You can always talk about work, but if you do you'll miss an opportunity to get to know the personal side of people. Besides, most people want to relax and have fun in those situations. So we're left with having to make small talk. It is such a big problem for people and yet the paradox about small talk is that it doesn't require that you do a lot of talking at all. The secret to good small talk is being a good listener. You simply need to ask a few open-ended questions to get the person talking. Then listen very carefully so that you can question them further and keep the conversation from dipping into awkward lulls. People love to talk about themselves and they'll appreciate your moving the conversation along. This is not difficult to do, but you will feel more comfortable if you prepare for the event in advance. Before your next work-related social event, complete the following exercise:

> Brainstorm a list of topics that you feel comfortable talking about. They can include a variety of subjects, e.g., current events, work, hobbies, books, vacations, or movies. Let your imagination run wild. It is not unusual for many folks to come up with at least thirty items. **(Success Step 1.4)**

Success Step 1.4 | Small Talk Exercise

Success Step

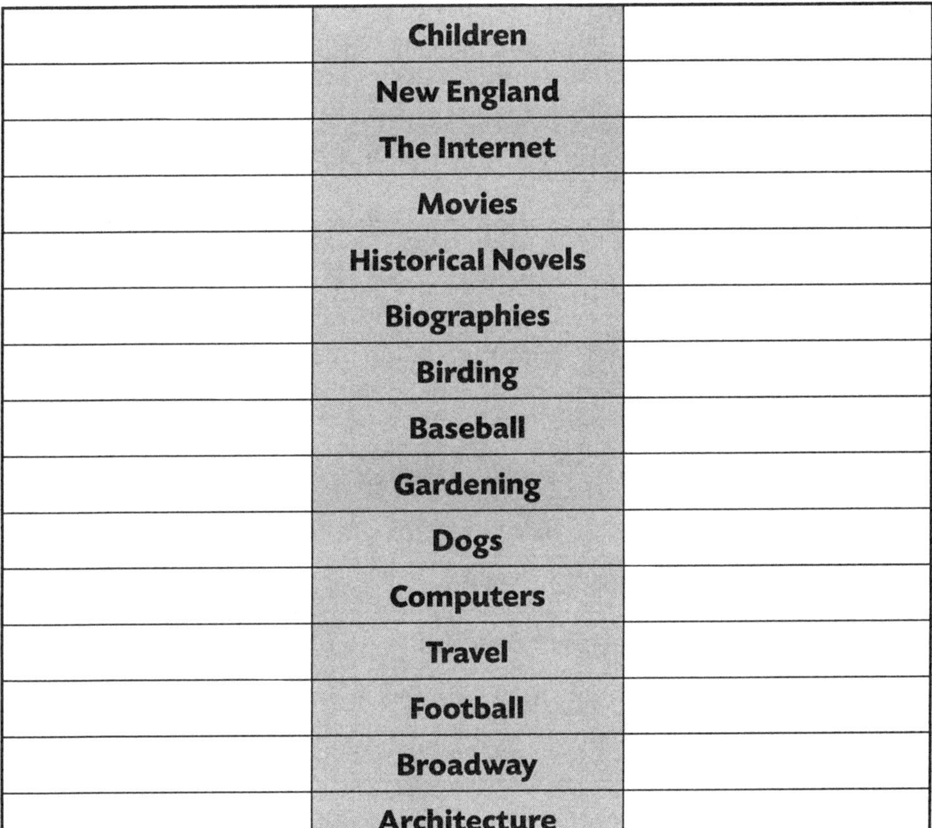

	Children	
	New England	
	The Internet	
	Movies	
	Historical Novels	
	Biographies	
	Birding	
	Baseball	
	Gardening	
	Dogs	
	Computers	
	Travel	
	Football	
	Broadway	
	Architecture	

Once your list is completed, reduce the items by half. Remove the topics that are religious, political, or controversial in nature as well as subjects so obscure that most people would not have an interest in them. (**Success Step 1.5**)

Success Step

Success Step 1.5 | Small Talk Exercise

	Children	
	New England	
	The Internet	
	Movies	
	Historical Novels	
	Biographies	
	Birding	
	Baseball	
	Gardening	
	Dogs	

Now rank each of the remaining items according to the following instructions:

> Place an "A" on the left side of the item that you believe would have the greatest amount of interest to others. Take your best guess. Now, identify the item that you feel would be of the second greatest interest to others and assign it a "B" ranking. Keep going in this manner until each item on your list has been ranked and the last item is of least interest to others. **(Success Step 1.6)**

Success Step 1.6 | Small Talk Exercise

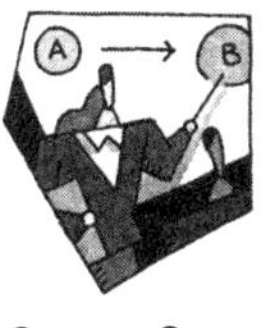

Success Step

B	**Children**	
E	**New England**	
A	**The Internet**	
G	**Movies**	
D	**Historical Novels**	
F	**Biographies**	
I	**Birding**	
H	**Baseball**	
C	**Gardening**	
J	**Dogs**	

Take a sheet of paper and cover up your ranking. Now review the list again. This time you are going to identify the item that is the easiest for you to talk about. On the right side of the item write the number "1." Find the next easiest subject to talk about and assign it the number "2," and so on. The last item to be ranked should be the most difficult for you to discuss. If you prefer to start with the hardest and work to the easiest, be my guest. **(Success Step 1.7)**

Success Step

Success Step 1.7 | Small Talk Exercise

B	**Children**	**1**
E	**New England**	**6**
A	**The Internet**	**5**
G	**Movies**	**9**
D	**Historical Novels**	**8**
F	**Biographies**	**3**
I	**Birding**	**10**
H	**Baseball**	**2**
C	**Gardening**	**4**
J	**Dogs**	**7**

Write out the numbers along with their corresponding letters. Now evaluate what you have (**Success Step 1.8**).

Success Step 1.8 | Small Talk Exercise

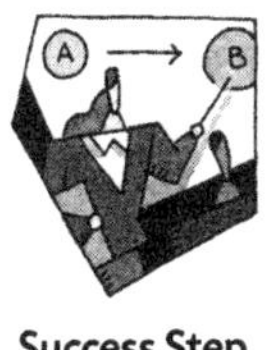

Success Step

✔			✔	✔					
1	2	3	4	5	6	7	8	9	10
B	H	F	C	A	E	J	D	G	I

In some cases you may find that the items that are most difficult for you to talk about are of little interest to others (see **Success Step 1.8**). Needless to say, we will scratch those items off the list. It could also be that those that are of greatest interest to others are the ones that are most difficult for you to discuss. In this case you may need to learn more about those topics so you can engage in these conversations more easily.

Choose three items that are of relatively high interest to others and fairly easy for you to talk about. In the example above, we've chosen the following three:

Children | Gardening | The Internet

You must now prepare to *not talk* about these items but to *ask questions* about them. Once you've identified the three items, jot down three open-ended questions related to that topic. For example, let's say the item is Gardening. Possible questions could be: Did you plant bulbs this season? How do you manage the garden maintenance with your busy schedule? Do you plant vegetables, flowers or both?

These questions are simple conversation starters. You should be able to walk into a social situation with at least nine of them (three per topic). I guarantee you will not ask one person all nine. You'll ask one or two and then, assuming that you are applying good listening skills, you should be able to ask enough questions to keep the conversation moving. Your objective is *not* to tell how much *you* know about the topic, but to learn and understand what the other person thinks about it. Remember, you want to demonstrate an interest in the other person. If you want to talk, wait to be invited. Let them ask you a question.

On occasion, you'll come across people who are very shy. Conversing with them is like pulling teeth. In this situation, you may have to do a little more chatting to fill up some airtime. But for the most part, if you're listening effectively, you'll have few problems in this area.

Learning from someone who plays the game well

Why does playing the game have such a bad rap? Perhaps it's because it is so easy to identify negative people that perpetuate this pessimistic perception. Nevertheless, I am confident that there are good people in your organization who play the game from a position of integrity, honesty, and respect for others.

> On a sheet of paper, list seven to ten attributes of a person who plays the game with integrity. (See **Success Step 1.9** on the next page.) When listing these behaviors, include things like: a good listener, a good sense of humor, trustworthy, and credible.

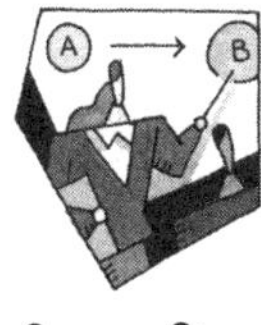

Success Step

Success Step 1.9 | Mr./Ms. Integrity

List behaviors and characteristics they demonstrate when playing the game.

1.	
2.	
3.	
4.	
5.	
6.	
7.	
8.	
9.	
10.	

Remember the list that you completed at the beginning of this chapter **(Success Step 1.1)**? You identified seven to ten reasons why you dislike playing the game. Compare it with your current list. Usually, these two lists are very different from each other. Can you see how we too often tend to focus on negatives as opposed to positives? It is not necessary to play the game the way the people on the first list play. You have now identified professionals who have more positive ways of playing the game and you can pattern your behavior after theirs.

I'd like you to review your current list of positive behaviors from Success Step 1.9 and copy them onto Success Step 1.10. Now review each item and think about how effective you are regarding that behavior or skill compared to the pro. In other words, assuming that the pro is a ten in every area, on that same scale of 1 to 10, where do you rank?

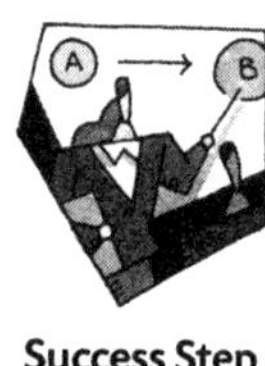

Success Step

Success Step 1.10 | Positive Behaviors of the Pros

Behaviors, Traits and Characteristics	1	2	3	4	5	6	7	8	9	10
A	•	•	•	•	•	•	•	•	•	•
B	•	•	•	•	•	•	•	•	•	•
C	•	•	•	•	•	•	•	•	•	•
D	•	•	•	•	•	•	•	•	•	•
E	•	•	•	•	•	•	•	•	•	•
F	•	•	•	•	•	•	•	•	•	•
G	•	•	•	•	•	•	•	•	•	•
H	•	•	•	•	•	•	•	•	•	•
I	•	•	•	•	•	•	•	•	•	•
J	•	•	•	•	•	•	•	•	•	•

Rate yourself on each of the attributes by placing a dot at the appropriate place on the continuum. Now connect the dots. You should have a jagged vertical line and a graphic representation of how developed a game player you are compared to the pro (see **Success Step 1.11** below). The space to the right of the line represents your potential or how far you have to go. The space to the left of the line represents how far you have come.

Success Step

Success Step 1.11 | Rate Yourself

Behaviors, Traits and Characteristics	1	2	3	4	5	6	7	8	9	10
A. *Sense of humor*	•	•	•	•	•	•	•	⬤	•	•
B. *Good listener*	•	•	•	•	⬤	•	•	•	•	•
C. *Ability to relate to diverse populations*	•	•	•	•	•	•	⬤	•	•	•
D. *Always buttoned up*	•	•	•	•	•	⬤	•	•	•	•
E. *Do what I say I will do*	•	•	•	•	•	•	•	•	⬤	•
F. *Have friends/contacts around the organization*	•	•	•	•	•	⬤	•	•	•	•
G. *Excellent track record*	•	•	•	•	•	•	•	•	⬤	•
H. *Understand the business*	•	•	•	⬤	•	•	•	•	•	•
I. *Personable*	•	•	•	•	•	•	⬤	•	•	•
J. *Ethical*	•	•	•	•	•	•	•	•	•	⬤

Now identify the one or two points furthest to the right and put a circle around them. Here's where you get a chance to pat yourself on the back. Congratulations! These are your strengths. Now identify the one or two points furthest to the left and put a square around those. These are the areas that you'll need to focus on for the next six months in order to improve your ability to play the game.

If playing the game is still somewhat daunting for you then put that term out of your head. Your assignment, should you decide to accept it, is to *connect* with people. The mission is possible.

Personal action plan

Answer the question, "What can I do on a regular basis to connect with others and increase my influence?" Now complete the action plan by describing what you are going to be doing, with whom, and by when; over the next 30, 60, and 90 days (see **Success Step 1.12**). Be sure to include an accountability partner — someone who holds your feet to the fire to ensure that this gets done.

Your action plan may be to have three to four luncheons scheduled over the next 90 days. It may be that you develop your conversation starters within the next 30 days. You may have a plan to invite a few colleagues to your home for a holiday dinner within 60 days. What's most important is that you commit to these actions and become the best game player you possibly can.

Success Step 1.12 | Playing the Game Personal Action Plan

Action Plan

Accountability Partner:______________________________

What can I do to connect with others and increase my influence?

30 days from now:______________________________

____

____

60 days from now:______________________________

____

____

90 days from now:______________________________

____

____

CHAPTER 2
The Success Model

Developing confidence

How do you feel when watching a pro basketball player at the foul line after he misses the first of two free throws? If the player is on your team, you are likely to be thinking, *"This guy is a professional — why can't he just get the ball into the hoop?"* Now think about the reaction of the player's teammates. They walk over to where he is on the foul line and give him an encouraging high-five. Why? They're boosting his confidence.

The term "playing with confidence" is often used to describe athletes who play well after having gone through a slump or after surviving an injury. In the world of sports, it is well understood that talent and skill, while important, are not enough. Players also need confidence to be successful. In the workplace, confidence is just as important.

A few years ago, I saw a TV commercial promoting the National Spelling Bee. The announcer was encouraging viewers to tune in because the youngsters participating represented "...today's great minds, tomorrow's leaders." The organizers were suggesting that since the contestants were gifted with great spelling abilities, they would be successful leaders in years to come. While I admired the copywriter's talent in coming up with such an effective sound bite, I wasn't convinced that a spelling bee is an accurate predictor of someone's leadership abilities. Nevertheless, this type of thinking — that your success is in large part determined by your innate ability — is prevalent in our society.

The Silver Spoon Model

Gifts + Talents = Success!

The Silver Spoon Model assumes that being born with a great talent or ability will make you successful. This thinking — that those who are smartest are the best — permeates our schools, the workplace, and even our families. It is not uncommon for teachers to group young children into ability groups as early as first grade. Parents and family members purchase computers and books for children who demonstrate intellectual gifts. College graduates from the best and the brightest schools are brought into organizations and identified as fast trackers or high-potentials. They are put into special rotational programs so that they can gain more knowledge, more quickly, and as a result, rise more rapidly to the highest levels of achievement.

The public sector is not terribly different. Perhaps you will recall when George W. Bush was running for president that there were many questions about his intellect. Many people were concerned that he was not bright enough to handle the job.

Ironically, there is no correlation between one's IQ and one's ability to lead or to be successful in life. Daniel Goleman in his book, *Emotional Intelligence,* suggests that IQ "...is not a guarantee of prosperity, prestige, or happiness in life...at best, IQ contributes about 20 percent of the factors that determine life success, which leaves 80 percent to other forces." (Goleman, Bantam Books, 1995)

When we study IQ and the general population, we see that only about fifteen percent of the population is considered "above average." Under the Silver Spoon Model, only a small group of people would qualify for the highest levels of positioning and title in our society, and approximately eighty-five percent of the people in this country would be dubbed ill-equipped to succeed.

The Success Model

If success were largely determined by genetics, then how do you explain the following example?

> *Imagine that I could create two young women who shared the exact same genetic material. They're clones, so absolutely everything about them is the same. They begin their careers in the workplace at the same time.*
>
> *Clone Number One arrives early every day so she can spend time with key people who also arrive early. She wants to learn as much as she can from them. She doesn't mind staying late to get the job done. She also takes classes in the evening; she reads incessantly, and makes every attempt to understand the job, the organization, and the industry. Clone Number Two leaves on time even when the workload is heavy. She does not go out of her way to attend classes, meet people, go to seminars or workshops, nor does she work particularly hard at learning the business or the organization.*

Which woman will be successful? Of course, the answer is Clone Number One. She is going to be successful because she is *determined* to be successful. We see then that success is not solely based on ability, gifts, and talents, but on determination: Sheer Determination.

Sheer Determination ➡ Success

Think about a time when you were successful in a particular area of your life. Your achievement was most likely something you worked very hard at. You were determined to succeed. Sheer Determination involves first making a decision about what you want, then being *disciplined* about how you're going to get there, and finally having the *drive*, *energy*, and *focus* to make it happen.

Do you know any successful people? I am sure they are both very smart and very talented. But I am equally certain that their success came as a result of very hard work. These successful people likely set goals and designed and executed strategies in a disciplined way to achieve their success. Taking your innate talents to their highest level requires your determination to work at it — Silver Spoons are not enough.

What drives Sheer Determination?

If all we had to do to be successful was to work hard and discipline ourselves, why aren't more people more successful more often? What is it that drives and ignites determination — the desire, the willingness, and the energy — to be successful? The answer is simply a Confident Attitude. It is the belief and faith that you can do what it takes to achieve success.

Confident Attitude* ➡ *Sheer Determination* ➡ *Success

I once saw a speaker exhorting a very large group of women to become more confident in their work lives and with their families. The speaker cocked her head, flipped her hair, threw her shoulders back and did a bit of a strut across the stage to demonstrate what confidence looks like. I wish we could put on a Confident Attitude as easily as putting on a hat. Unfortunately, you can cock your head, strut your stuff, twirl around, jump up and down and you will have no more confidence than when you began. A cocky attitude is not confidence.

Where does a Confident Attitude come from?

Confidence is born out of your experience with success. (See **Illustration 2.1**) Your successful outcomes are the result of your strong *desire* or determination to be successful. Your belief and faith in yourself *drive* your level of determination. The greater and more frequent your success, the more your confidence is strengthened. Stronger levels of faith, belief, and confidence allow you to muster even greater determination, *discipline* and focus — leading to increasingly higher levels of success.

Illustration

Illustration 2.1 | The Success Model

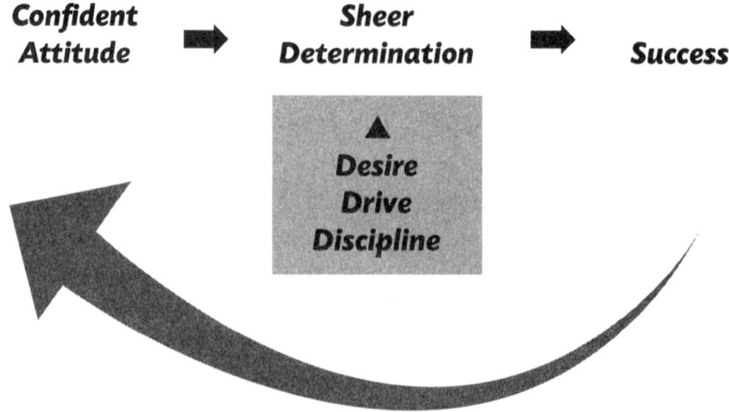

What do we need to be successful in the workplace?
Most people are not without any confidence; they have confidence in some area or another. However, to be successful in the workplace, you need three types of confidence: intellectual confidence, social confidence, and political confidence. (See **Illustration 2.2**)

Intellectual confidence. Many people go into the workplace with intellectual confidence, particularly if they have been to college or some other form of higher education. They're confident in this area because they have had experience applying themselves to intellectual pursuits. They know they can learn and they believe they're smart, so these kinds of activities don't intimidate them. They are confident that they can negotiate in this arena. This type of confidence, while important, is not enough to be successful in the workplace.

Social confidence. You need social confidence, or the ability to influence and relate well to people. If you tend to avoid social situations at work or when you do attend feel less than confident, you probably need to strengthen and hone your social skills. We offer many ideas on how to manage the social arena at work in Chapter 1.

Political confidence. Many people are unprepared for the political dimension that exists in the workplace and they show it by saying things like, "I don't do politics. That's just not me," or "I just want my work to speak for itself." This type of thinking is naïve and misguided. Participating in the political landscape of your workplace depends upon your understanding of it. And jumping into the game is the only way you will develop confidence in this area.

Illustration

Illustration 2.2

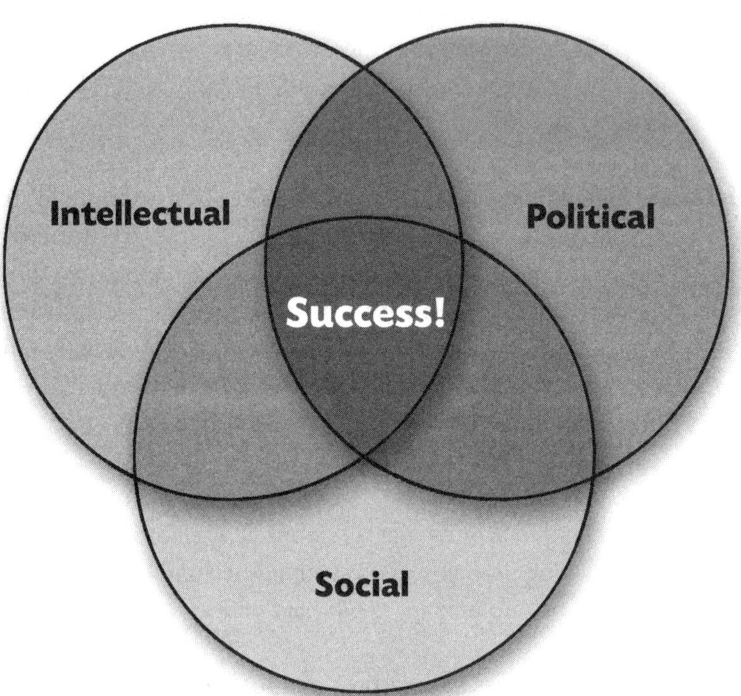

The above illustration demonstrates your need to be confident in all three areas to become successful. They're interconnected. You need intellectual and social skills to develop political skills and confidence. You need political skills and confidence to strengthen your confidence in the social and intellectual area. You may need to borrow from one area in order to strengthen another. For example, in a social situation where you feel less confident, you can draw from your intellectual confidence and your political abilities to strengthen your social skills. How? By directing the conversation to a subject you are comfortable discussing.

If you are going to develop confidence in any of these areas, you must develop a strategy. Successful outcomes will strengthen your confidence and unsuccessful outcomes will provide important feedback to help you plan more successful strategies in the future.

How can you strengthen and build your confidence?
There are three keys to building confidence: supportive relationships, a structured growth process, and healthy attributions.

Supportive relationships. No one achieves any significant level of success without supportive relationships from people within your family, your community, your place of worship, or workplace. These people act as your cheerleaders. They pick you up when you're down, give you a "go girl" or an "atta boy" when you've had a success. Sometimes, the people you develop these relationships with have succeeded in similar areas that you are aspiring to and are willing to both encourage and mentor you. Make sure you have people around you who believe in you.

A structured growth process. A structured growth process is a step-by-step plan whereby you achieve a goal and then incrementally take another, more challenging step, and then another. When I first started to lift weights, I recognized that I would not be successful doing bicep curls with fifteen-pound weights. So, I started with two-pound weights. Over a period of time I needed a greater challenge, so I picked up five-pound weights, then eight-pound weights, then ten and twelve. Before I knew it, I was able to handle the fifteen-pounders! Not only had my muscles become stronger, so had my confidence.

Healthy attributions. Keeping our confidence strong and healthy is, in part, dependent on what we say about our successes and our failures. Research tells us that confident people make attributions that keep their confidence intact, and that people who lack confidence make attributions that do nothing to protect their confidence.

Let's see how that works.

Jessica is a talented corporate trainer with a high degree of confidence when it comes to her ability to speak before a group. When she has assignments, she generally works very hard to prepare by doing her homework and practicing. Once she has delivered a successful program and has a chance to reflect on her performance, her thought process might sound something like this: "Boy, I am good (innate ability) and I worked hard (effort)." Because these attributions are internal, Jessica's confidence is strengthened and so are her expectations about future success.

Jessica is not perfect and occasionally will experience a program that bombs. As she reflects upon a performance that most would agree was a failure, this is her thought process. "If I am going to be effective, I am going to have to buckle down, work harder, smarter and more strategically. I'll work through this" (effort).

When confident people like Jessica experience failure, they stay focused on their lack of appropriate effort. Perhaps they did not consider the political consequences, or apply enough strategic or creative thinking. Maybe they just didn't talk to the right people, or were not disciplined or motivated. Whatever the reason for the failure, they stay focused on their lack of appropriate effort. Effort is internal to us and it is within our control (see **Illustration 2.3**). Confident people believe they can rework the situation and their confidence remains intact.

When confident people experience success they attribute that success to their ability and their effort. These attributions are *internal* to them so their confidence is strengthened and so are their expectations about future success. People who attribute their success to areas that are *external* to them (e.g., task difficulty) lack confidence, as those attributions do nothing to strengthen their confidence. Their attributions sound like "Oh, it was easy…anybody could do that." Or, "the sun and the planets were properly lined up and I got lucky today." These attributions do nothing to strengthen their confidence because they base their success on *external* events. Their expectations for future success are lower than those of confident people who make healthy attributions.

> *Jim is a quiet, shy person who is comfortable in the world of his own thoughts and ideas. He is most uncomfortable speaking before groups of people; he avoids them and, as a result, he lacks public speaking confidence. When Jim is asked to deliver a presentation, he prepares well and does a good job. His reflections on his performance may sound like this: "Whew! They liked me, I'm so lucky." Or, "They liked me, but anybody could have done it."*

Jim is attributing his success to factors that are *external* to him and hence cannot strengthen his confidence.

> *When Jim experiences the dreaded public speaking failure, i.e., the bomb, his reflections on his performance may sound like: "I knew I couldn't do it."*

People who lack confidence attribute their failures to their lack of ability.

Illustration 2.3 | Attribution Theory

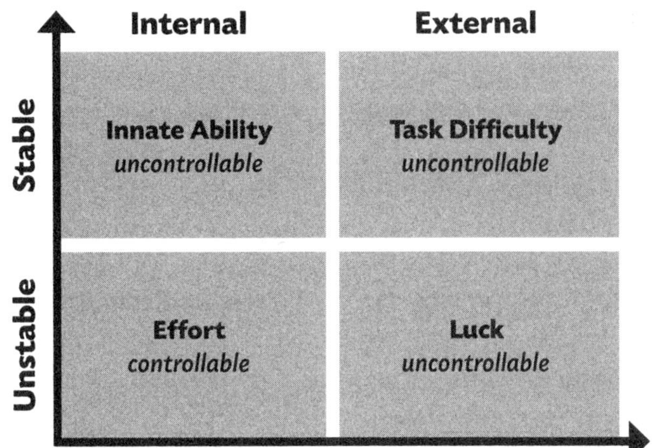

Illustration

When you say things like, "I'm just not good at computers," and you believe that you lack some innate ability in working with computers, you're stuck! You have just convinced yourself that when it comes to computers, there's nothing you can do. On the other hand, if you say to yourself, "I've got to work harder to learn more about how to operate computers," then you are more likely to achieve success.

Listen to yourself and bite your tongue when you make unhealthy attributions. Focus on attributing your success to your ability and to your effort. Similarly, attribute your lack of success to the lack of appropriate effort.

I'd like to take a "coaching moment" and address those of you who are leaders. Athletic coaches completely understand the relationship between confidence and success. When the team is going through a slump, it is the coach's job to encourage the players and build their confidence. As a result, good coaches create stronger, more effective teams. Hometown fans also help to pump up a team. Teams are more likely to win at home than on the road because they are surrounded by thousands of supportive people who are rooting for them. The fans believe in their team, the players believe in themselves, and they play better.

I believe the most important aspect of your role as a leader is to build and strengthen the confidence of your people. If they believe in you, and believe that you believe in them, you can take them to untold heights of performance and productivity. Make certain they are continually engaged in a process of growth; that you're encouraging them and helping them to realize their potential.

Confidence is the key — *yours and theirs.*

Success Step 2.1 | Action Plan

Action Plan

1. Are you equally confident in all three areas of confidence? ____________________

2. In which area of confidence could you be more confident? ____________________

3. Identify 2-3 actions you can take to increase your effort and confidence:

____

____

____

____

____

____

____

____

CHAPTER 3
Goal Setting for Success

Recently, my college roommate was in town for a few days. As we reflected on old times and how life has treated us, Mary made a statement that I thought was very profound.

"I'm tired of always feeling stuck in life," she said matter-of-factly.
"What do you mean?" I asked.
"I feel like I'm going through the motions but nothing is happening."
"Well, do you have any goals?" I asked.

After she confirmed my suspicions that she, in fact, had been drifting along without having set goals, I shared with Mary what I consider to be a profound truth. People who write goals and allow them to influence their lives do not live in the type of imperviousness she described.

We relaxed and spent the next few hours examining major areas of her life and wrote her goals. I volunteered to type Mary's goals and send them to her when she returned to her home.

When I called Mary to be sure that she had received her list of goals, I was thrilled to learn how much progress she had made. In those few short weeks, and without a hard copy of the goals, Mary had internalized her goals. The process had shifted from an intellectual exercise to one she embraced wholly — within her soul — mind, body, and spirit.

Mary's story is typical of many people. As a Leadership Development coach for over 20 years, I have been privileged to work with hundreds of talented men and women to increase their influence and their impact. In spite of their extraordinary gifts, far too many have no goals. They are continually reacting to the winds of life. As a result, they're left feeling frustrated and unfulfilled. They lack the power and control that goal setting provides.

In a workshop setting, I am very surprised if more than 20 percent of the participants affirm they have written goals. The vast majority of people are adrift in the sea of life, getting tossed and jostled about by the whims of nature.

Goal setting allows you to connect with your dreams, to set a course, and then to navigate toward them. Certainly you'll hit a few storms and face tough times. But having written goals to guide you will ensure that you are traveling toward your specified destination. Checking and rechecking the progress of your navigational systems — or the steps you take in the direction of your dreams — will most assuredly get you there.

Goal setting is the single, most powerful factor in achieving success in life. Surely you know people who have achieved success beyond your imagination. What's the difference between those people and you? Are they smarter, more talented, or more educated? Probably not. The difference is that they wanted success so much that they were willing to translate their dreams into goals and strategies and put their plans into action. Goal setting is life's elixir to unblocking fears, doubts, and confusion about the future. It helps you create a life of free-flowing opportunities, satisfaction, and fulfillment.

For more than 20 years, I have been serious about writing my goals. I've been able to look back over each year's list to examine areas in my life where I have grown, areas where I've missed the mark, and to see, in black and white, the reasons why. Understanding why I've missed goals is important to me. It helps me avoid unnecessary guilt, make proper adjustments for the future, and determine whether the missed goal should maintain a viable place on my list of priorities or not.

Goals in the midst of life's challenges

Sometimes circumstances change, and sometimes you change. Things that were once important to you when you were younger become less important. And things that did not seem important ten years ago suddenly become very significant. We often miss the mark in reaching our goals because we've either failed to pay enough attention to them or lacked the proper resources to see them to fruition. There are any number of things that can prevent us from achieving our goals.

I have no crystal ball that helps me see the future, but I've lived long enough to know that life will serve up a few surprises, obstacles, and a variety of twists and turns at some point or another. It's like flying through turbulence — which can be an unsettling and frightening experience. When an airline captain requests that passengers keep their seatbelts fastened, some people simply relax and go with the movement of the plane. They understand that the bumpy ride is temporary and that smooth sailing is invariably on the other side of the turbulence. These people have a sense of control, not of the plane, but of their reaction to what is going on around them.

Other passengers become fearful and fight the movement. They can't see beyond the temporary situation because they choose to focus on the fear of what "might" happen. They feel a loss of control and experience tremendous anxiety. What they fail to realize is that normal turbulence, though disconcerting, does not take the plane off course. Nor does severe turbulence, for that matter. Rather, it causes the plane to adjust its course in search of smoother air while continuing toward the planned destination.

Similarly, goals ensure that you are on a proper trajectory and that life's turbulence won't take you off course. It may slow you down and cause you to make some adjustments, but ultimately you will arrive at your destination.

Goal setting is an extremely powerful tool. Given the vast number of things in life that are outside our control, it is always to our benefit to control the things that we can. Goal setting allows us to identify what's important and to effect change. As a result, the probability of our success increases.

If you are not interested in achieving success in your career or in some other area of your life — be it finances, health, family, or education — that's fine. You don't have to set goals. If you want to be financially secure, manage your time well, enjoy healthy relationships, a satisfying career, and good health, then you don't have a choice — goal setting is the best route to getting you there. Now, have a seat and let's get started.

You reap what you sow

I love to garden. I live in a place where the winters can be lengthy and severe. After a long season of gray skies, bare trees, black ice and dirty snow, spring flowers mean so much to me. As soon as the first crocus begins to peek through the snow, I feel a deep sense of satisfaction in my soul that all is well in the world. But to ensure that I experience God's handiwork in the spring, I must be a full participant and do my part in the fall. I plant bulbs. When I want a greener lawn in the spring, I treat the grass by adding lime in the fall. When I want a richer soil, because the secret of great gardening is great soil, I add mulch in the fall. When I want to ensure that the more delicate shrubs and trees survive the winter, I protect them in the fall.

Can you guess when I like to write my goals? You got it! I write them in the fall. Actually, there's no good or bad time to write goals. Many people like to write goals around the New Year, others write them on birthdays. My husband and I take a day off each year to discuss our household goals. We go to our favorite restaurant, enjoy a great lunch, and spend about three hours discussing our kids, leaky roofs, vacations, and decks that need painting. It's fun and very productive. I think all couples should take at least one day a year to discuss and plan things that affect them as a couple and as a family.

I like to write my personal and business goals in November because it's a good time to reflect on what has happened over the past year. And it gives me plenty of time before the New Year to fine-tune them.

Whatever time you choose to write your goals is up to you. The important thing is that you stick to the dates, and you actually get down to the business of goal setting.

Experienced gardeners will tell you how important it is to prepare the soil before you plant. You have to create an environment in which the seeds can germinate, take root, and get nourishment in order to thrive. I like to write goals in an environment that I find stimulating and nurturing. I could certainly go into my office, sit at my desk, and type my goals on my computer. That would work. But to stimulate my thinking and to remove the natural limitations of my structured work environment, I like to do something a little more exotic.

Personal sacrifices

For the past ten years I've traveled to Bermuda with about 20 other independent consultants for a Strategic Planning Retreat. We meet formally for three intense half-days to discuss our businesses. It is not easy to ignore the beautiful blue water and lush vegetation, but somehow we do. We identify what has happened to our goals during the previous year and set our goals for the next year.

By the end of the retreat, my goals for the upcoming year have been written, shared, tweaked, critiqued, and blessed by trusted professionals. These reliable colleagues function as my personal Board of Directors, offering guidance and support throughout the year. It is the most powerful and important thing that I do for my business each year.

I attend professional conferences and workshops throughout the year so I can learn new strategies and grow in my field. I read books and magazines that are relevant to my work. But I would not risk going into the New Year without going through the analysis that the Bermuda event requires of me.

Just what is so magical about Bermuda? Why do I invest my resources to travel to this wonderful part of the world each year? Does that blue-green water hold some mystical properties? Do my colleagues have crystal balls? Are they more intelligent, gifted, and special in some way? Yes, they are pretty special. But the "magic" is not in the trip at all. It is in the goal setting process itself. You really don't need to travel anywhere special. Three or four personal friends or family members gathered around your kitchen table can work well as an effective Board of Directors as long as they sincerely care about your growth and development.

It is very nice to do this kind of work in a beautiful environment. But what is most important is to find an environment where you can shut out distractions. You may find the local library works best for you, or that sitting on a park bench or near a lake is the environment you need. The most important thing, though, is to find it!

Abracadabra

There's an old story about John F. Kennedy many of you are probably familiar with. A group of researchers conducted a longitudinal study on his graduating class from Harvard. They determined that the graduates who were most successful 20 years later were not the ones with the highest GPAs. They weren't those that had family money or political connections. In fact, they were those young men who had vision concerning their futures. They wrote their goals and then went to work at making them happen. Getting your goals onto paper *is* the magical formula.

I discovered this "magic" in my own life a little over 20 years ago when I was training to be an Executive Coach. One of my homework assignments required that I write specific actions that I could and would do to achieve a set of objectives. I wrote them, checked them out with my Master Coach, and filed them. One year later I retrieved them and was pleased to see how much I had accomplished, even though I hadn't revisited them. I had achieved most of these goals with seemingly little effort. Another exercise required that I write my Vision of Success. I was to project what my life would look like in 20 years in terms of finances, career, family, geographical location, and material possessions. I wrote a vision that I thought was a bit of a stretch and a bit fanciful. After discussing it with my Master Coach, I filed it.

When I reviewed it four years later, I was amazed. I had achieved *80 percent* of what I had written. At this point I became a believer and was totally hooked on the power of writing goals.

It may appear that I'm suggesting you only need to write your goals and they will "magically" happen. Frankly, it does feel this way at times. But the reality is that things don't just happen. Getting your goals on paper increases the probability of your success because it causes you to crystallize your thinking. Your goals become embedded in your subconscious and create a mindset that leads you toward achieving them. As a result, you find yourself making decisions and becoming attracted to people, places, and things that facilitate the achievement of those goals. There's nothing spooky going on in the universe. The planets don't have to line up in a particular way. It's simply and powerfully your ability to focus on what you want and to consciously and unconsciously work to make your dreams come true.

There are some steps and processes that you can put into place to further increase your probability of success.

Going public

When I decided to write this book, I announced it at the Bermuda event to my entire group of colleagues and peers. My voice was shaky and quiet but I said it nevertheless. I knew that I when I returned the following year I had to be in position to report on my success. I outlined a plan that would allow me to complete the work within a year. (I occasionally read that plan when I want a good laugh.) The following year when I retuned to Bermuda I did not have a book in tow but I was well on the way. The year after I returned having completed the book and with the publisher's contract.

The probability of your success increases when you write your goals. It increases even more when you write them down *and* make them public. I'm not suggesting that you take out an advertisement in your local newspaper or television station. Rather, take advantage of opportunities to share your goals with your family, friends, and trusted colleagues.

I have to admit that going public, in the beginning, made me very uncomfortable. Many years ago, I wanted to learn to facilitate a particular program and offer it to clients. In a meeting with 50 other professionals, I put that dream on the table. I'm not sure anyone heard what I was saying because I mumbled and spoke very softly. In spite of my awkwardness, I managed to get the words out of my mouth. Three months later I achieved my goal. It was pretty amazing.

Part of the reason for my traveling to Bermuda each year is that it satisfies the requirement of going public. Even though I'm sharing my goals with people I trust, who care about the success of my business, I'm still putting myself on the line.

Another benefit of going public is that your goals are put into the heads of other people who can support you with resources and ideas related to what you're trying to accomplish. At this point, achieving your goals becomes a team approach. It's just that the other players are not aware that they've been drafted onto your team. It's very exciting.

One component of the "magic" is what I call "noodling." I define noodling as the process of modifying, tweaking, and making sure your goals are as clear and workable as possible. After writing my goals in November, I look for and take advantage of all opportunities to refine my goals. This means getting input from others and making sure my calculations and projections are on target. I really enjoy this part of the process.

The first year after the September 11th attack, I found myself, like so many others, searching to add deeper meaning to what I do and who I am. I felt a strong need to add a spiritual component to my goal setting process. I traveled to Miami to meet with three other women who are also independent consultants. Our objectives were to discuss and pray about our businesses.

I went to Miami with the goals I had written in Bermuda. I wanted to focus on one goal in particular — writing this book. At this point, I had written a book proposal and I wanted to take it public in Miami.

We began our mini-retreat on Friday evening with dinner, where we outlined how we would spend our time together. The next day we dedicated an hour to focus on each woman's business — her goals and her challenges. The following morning was spent in prayer and reflection.

Going public showed me that my book proposal was crammed with ideas that could fill two, maybe three books. Here's where the process of noodling was so helpful. I decided to streamline my thoughts and write the proposal around a central theme.

I had been feeling a need to disconnect from certain activities and relationships so that I could spend more time focusing on the book, my business, and other important areas of my life. This desire to cut off the old and honor the new made me uncomfortable. I felt a bit egotistical as I mentally crossed people off my "I just don't have time for *them* anymore" list. I mean, who did I think I was? But, again, the process of going public with this goal, noodling it with trusted friends, and spending time with God, gave me both the tools and the confidence to fulfill my goals. It was a powerful time of insight and direction.

The process of goal setting and noodling can be challenging; you don't have to travel to Miami or Berumda to accomplish them. You simply have to grab pen and paper, create an environment of serenity, and make it happen.

Follow the yellow brick road

Life would be a lot easier if we could skip our way down a predetermined path that would lead us to our destiny. I know of some characters who attempted to do just that, except they lacked a few essentials. The fact is that we *can* walk through life on a type of yellow brick road — one that is defined by our goals. The City of Oz is our Vision of Success and establishing goals to get there is the pathway, or yellow brick road. Don't let anyone fool you: it takes a lot of heart, courage, and brains.

Vision of Success

How do you define your Vision of Success? I mentioned earlier that my first stab at it required me to look forward 20 years. That's pretty far and, depending on your age and what's meaningful for you, may or may not make sense. The good news about writing a 20-year vision is that you don't have to do very much today to get started on it. The bad news is that it may not be as motivating as a vision that is more short term.

If you'd like to start smaller, try writing a three-year vision or five-year or ten. If you're 43, you might look out to age 50. Do whatever is meaningful for you. Whatever time frame you choose, write it from your head *and* from your heart. You're working to map out a significant chunk of your life, so use both the right and left sides of your brain.

The best way to do this is through a process of visualization. Find a place where you feel totally comfortable and at peace. Once you've found a spot, close your eyes and allow your imagination to create a vision of what you would love your life to look like in the time frame you've identified. Picture the various aspects of your life, e.g., career, family, geographical location, and education and write down a few key words that describe the desires of your heart. (See **Success Step 3.1** on the next page.)

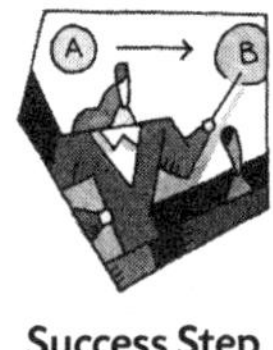

Success Step

Success Step 3.1 | Vision of Success

Long-Term Goals

Areas of Life	***In 3 years*** *What does your Vision look like in this area?*	***In 5 years*** *What does your Vision look like in this area?*	***In 10 years*** *What does your Vision look like in this area?*
Career			
Family			
Education/Training			
Financial			
Spiritual			
Community			
Social			
Health/Fitness			
Personal Goals (travel, etc.)			

Once you have the picture in mind, open your eyes and begin to write. Jot down as many details as you can. Don't let the left side of your brain — your reason and intellect — talk you out of what the right side of your brain — your creativity, emotions, and desires — would enjoy. I find that most people usually stay within what they can realistically achieve over a period of time.

The next step is to determine which goals you need to achieve in the short term in order to realize the long-term vision. (**Success Step 3.2**)

Success Step 3.2 | Vision of Success

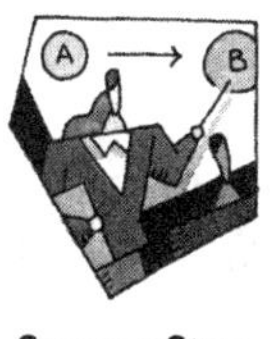

Success Step

Short-Term Goals

Important Areas of Your Life	***12-Month Goals***	***18-Month Goals***
Career		
Family		
Education/ Training		
Financial		
Spiritual		
Community		
Social		
Health/Fitness		
Personal Goals (travel, etc.)		

I'm not exactly sure why this is, but some folks find visualizing their future a rather daunting experience. If that's you, I have an easier approach that I learned from my dear friend and fellow coach, Joan Cutlip. It's called the "Wheel of Life."
(See **Illustration 3.1**)

Illustration

Illustration 3.1 | The Wheel of Life

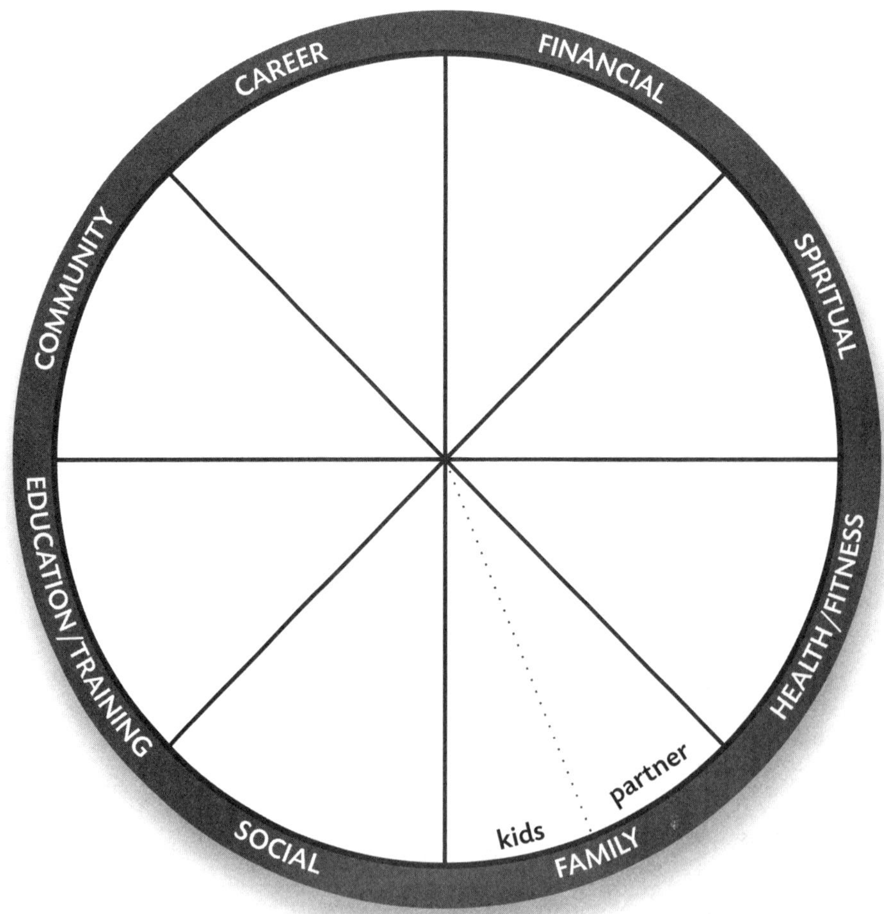

The pie chart wedges represent eight areas of your life: Career, Financial, Spiritual, Health/Fitness, Family, Social, Education/Training, Community. You may wish to divide "family" into two smaller wedges to represent different subgroups such as kids and spouse, or siblings and parents.

Fill in or shade each area to indicate your Current Level of Satisfaction. (See **Illustration** 3.2)

Illustration 3.2 | The Wheel of Life

Current Level of Satisfaction

Illustration

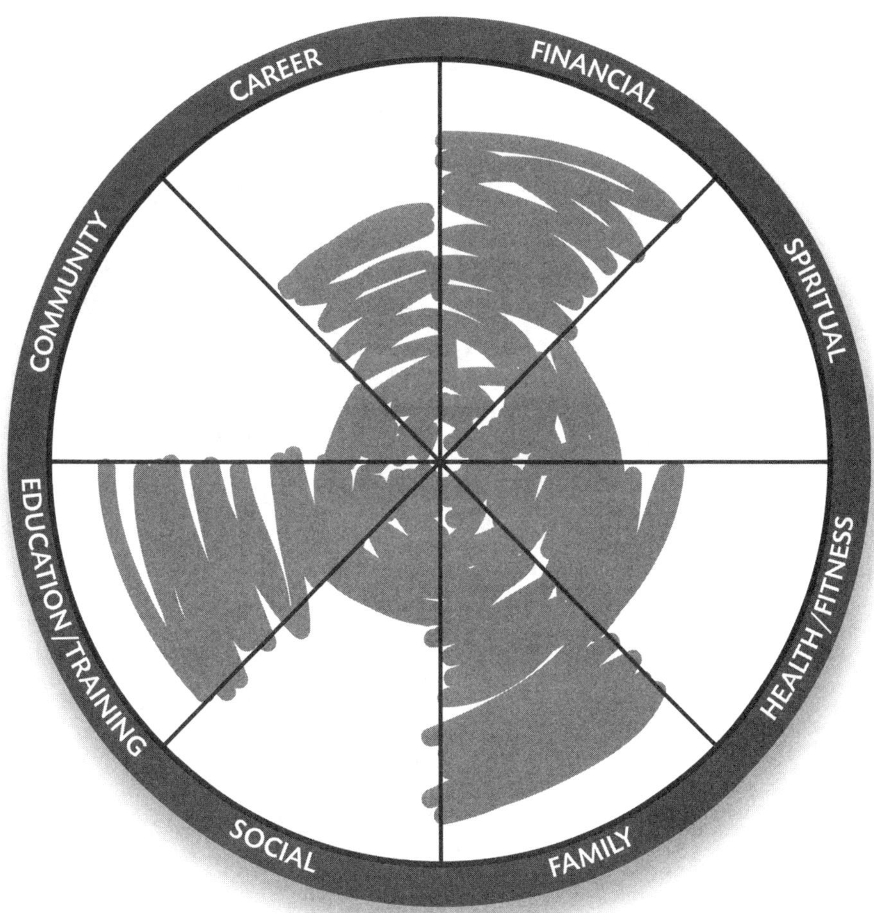

Now, with a different colored pen, shade the Desired Level of Satisfaction. (See **Illustration 3.3**)

Illustration

Illustration 3.3 | The Wheel of Life

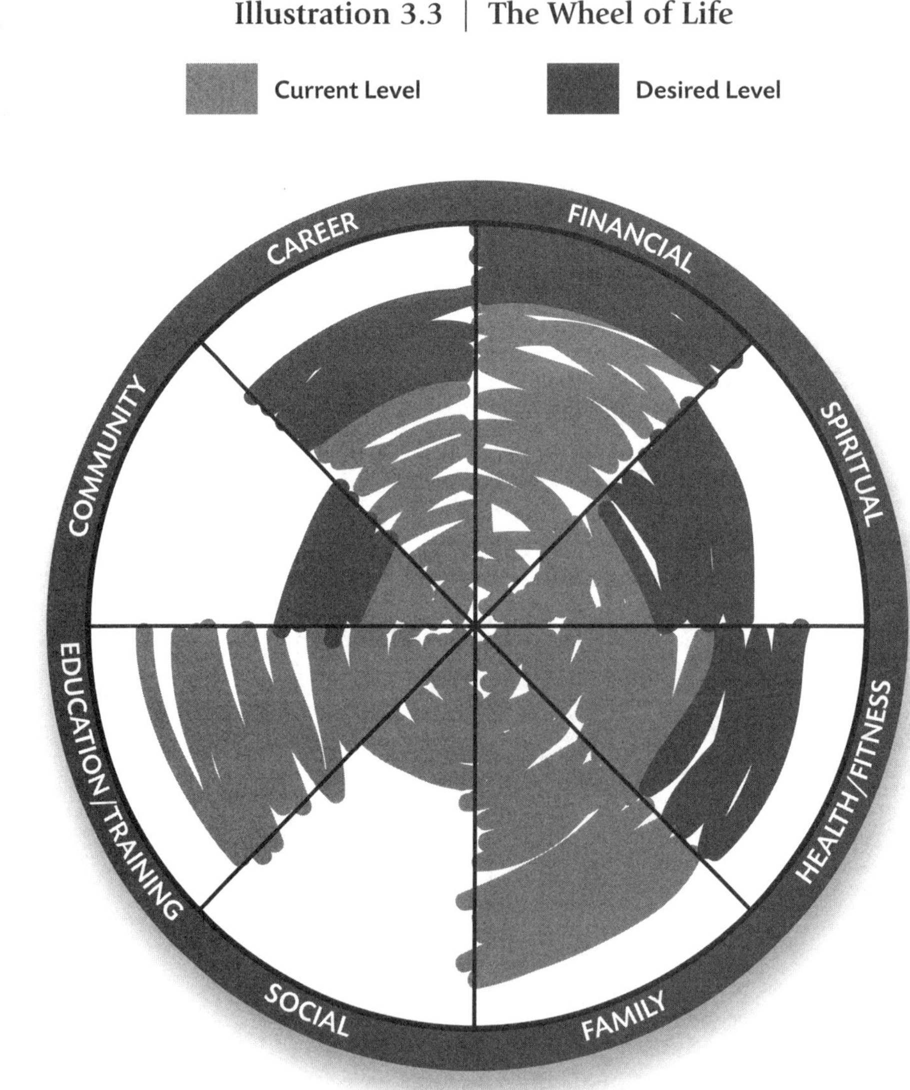

If the difference between your Current Level and Desired Level of Satisfaction is significant, you likely have an area that needs attention. You can bring these two levels of satisfaction into alignment by setting goals.

All wedges need not be completely filled in to indicate 100 percent desired satisfaction, but be honest with yourself. If you are not interested in or able to serve your community this year because your plate is full, it's okay. In fact, thinking this out in advance allows you to avoid any guilt you might feel when you have to decline a request to serve on a community board or church committee. We can't do everything, at least not at the same time. By all means remain flexible. But you must be very clear about what is important and meaningful for your life right now. Reviewing your "Wheel of Life" each year is a quick and easy way to measure progress.

S.M.A.R.T. goals

We've established that goal setting is important and that writing goals in the proper environment helps facilitate the process. Now let's talk turkey. Exactly how do we write them? Perhaps the most popular and well-known concept for writing goals is the S.M.A.R.T. model. A good goal that is poorly written is less likely to be achieved than a fair goal that is well written. A well-written goal should be Specific, Measurable, offer Accountability, and should be Realistic and Time-framed.

Specific

Goals must be specific so you can determine whether or not you've been successful. When a goal is too general you'll be hard pressed to know when you have achieved it because it has been ill-defined. For example, if your goal is "to be more successful," you have to define what "more successful" means to you. It could mean spending more time with your children, getting a promotion on the job, or achieving professional recognition.

Measurable

If you can't measure the goal, you won't know when and if you've been successful. If your goal is to spend more time with your children, you must determine how much time you spend with them now and how much more time you'll need to spend with them to feel successful.

Accountable

Identify a friend, colleague, or family member you feel comfortable with, and work out a schedule to discuss how you're coming along with your goals. Supportive relationships have been critical to my success in achieving goals. We'll say more about accountability in the next section.

Realistic

Achieving your dreams is certainly a part of the goal setting process. But if you want to achieve your goals, you'll need to stay within the realm of what is realistic. I'm a pretty good baseball player and I know how to write S.M.A.R.T. goals, but no matter how well I play or how well I write goals, it's not very likely that I will ever play for the New York Yankees.

Time Framed

Time frames keep you on track and accountable. A certain amount of reality is important here as well. Do you have the ability and willingness to commit the time required in order to achieve your goals? One of the biggest mistakes I see people make is to set goals that are realistic but too complex in relation to the demands on their time. Your accountability partners can help you decide if your timing makes sense.

Question: Do you know how to eat an elephant?
Answer: One bite at a time!

Break your goals into manageable parts and assign them appropriate time frames. You'll find achieving big goals to be an easier task.

Mirror, mirror on the wall

Because you're reading this book I assume that success is important to you. Let's talk about how you can "kick it up" a notch.

I'm pretty confident in my assumption that many of you enjoy a sense of control. So here's the paradox: to experience a sense of control in achieving results, you're actually going to have to give up a measure of control to someone else. In other words, you're going to ask someone to hold you accountable. Obviously you'll have to find the right person or persons; people you respect and trust to tell you the truth.

Working with your accountability partners at agreed upon times serves to keep your goals at a higher level of consciousness. Reviewing your goals throughout the year allows you to make mid-point corrections and modifications. There are goals that may have made a lot of sense in November, but six months later do not because circumstances have changed.

My daughter was in a near-fatal accident one spring. As a result, the goals I had set the prior November were mostly null and void. My circumstances had instantly and dramatically changed and so had my priorities.

Your accountability partner can be helpful when you're facing changing circumstances. There is something very affirming about having another person validate your decision when you have to eliminate or modify a goal. It takes away the guilt you may unnecessarily impose upon yourself for not completing that goal.

When an aircraft leaves New York en route to San Francisco, the pilots have a flight plan. The route is thoroughly mapped out and on-board computers are programmed to satisfy flight requirements. These men and women are highly trained and experienced, having logged countless flight-hours. How comfortable would you feel knowing that they had no intention of checking in with air-traffic controllers until they reached San Francisco? It is likely that most of us would not be comfortable with that at all.

There are many variables that affect a smooth and direct flight — weather, air traffic, mechanical difficulties, and terrorist threats. Mid-flight adjustments are inevitable. Pilots are required to check in with a flight tower several times during the flight to move safely along their route. If they fly into turbulence or a thunderstorm, plans may have to change. Pilots will fly at higher or lower altitudes to find smoother air, or laterally to avoid the storms. Even with the best of plans, the nonstop flight is not always possible. The pilot's accountability partner, the air traffic controller, ensures that the flight stays on course while taking into account the unavoidable and the unexpected.

You may consider having more than one accountability partner, e.g., one who focuses on your business goals and another who focuses on your personal goals. You might discuss your fitness goals with a personal trainer or a friend who shares your interest in fitness. If you work with a small team of accountability partners, think of them as your personal Board of Directors. They should provide you with support, ideas, encouragement, and a realistic assessment of how you're doing.

Scoring the game

When I'm at a baseball stadium, scoring the game in my scorebook, I record hits, strikes, errors, bases on balls, passed balls, and runs. It helps me understand what's going on at a more strategic level.

Monitoring your progress against goals is a very meaningful exercise. You can be very strategic in goal setting and very realistic in terms of what you can reasonably handle each year. However, if you don't achieve all your goals at the end of the year, you are not a loser; quite the contrary.

The object of the game is not to achieve each and every goal you set. There are too many variables that make the achievement of all your goals each year improbable. The process of setting yearly goals positions you to consistently advance at a pace that would not be possible without goals. In other words, if you're shooting for the stars and only hit the moon, you're still in a much better position than when you started.

As you advance closer and closer to your Vision of Success each year, you will experience the satisfaction and fulfillment of a successful life. I don't measure my success each year by how many goals I've achieved. My greatest achievement is in taking charge of my life and controlling and influencing what I can through the process of writing goals.

Action Plan

Success Step 3.3 | Action Plan

Schedule a time to complete the worksheets discussed in this chapter.

CHAPTER 4
Understanding Self and Others

Years ago, I was interviewing the director of a preschool for my three-year-old daughter Stacey. As I sat with her, observing the children, one child came to her and whined, "Bruce took my toy." She calmly bent over and said, "Go back and tell him, 'I don't like that. Please give me back my toy.'" She then turned to me and said, "Children just don't have the language for dealing with these kinds of situations and that's what they find frustrating."

I never forgot that little scene because I have seen it replayed many times among adults. I can't help but overhear people in the subway or at the bus stop complaining about the way a supervisor, customer, or colleague spoke to them. I've been in the ladies' room when women have come in weeping because of something "she" said.

We don't always know what to say or how to say things when we find ourselves at odds with someone. How many times have you walked away from a difficult situation frustrated, kicking yourself, wishing you had said this or said that? It is very difficult to know how to communicate our needs or feelings (the not-so-nice ones) without whining or coming across as hostile. Regardless of the difficulty in expressing ourselves, learning to communicate effectively is essential to your workplace success.

This chapter will help you confidently manage these situations in a way that protects you from receiving bad feelings, give you the tools to respond appropriately, and hold others accountable for their actions and decisions.

Milk and cookies anyone?

I'd like to begin this phase of our journey with the fictitious story of Sinbad and Abigail.

> *Abigail lived on one side of a river. Her boyfriend, Gregory, lived on the other. It had been several months since Abigail and Gregory had seen each other and her heart longed for him. Alas, she had no money to get to the other side.*
>
> *She took a short trip down to the local ferryboat and asked Sinbad, the Captain, if he could take her across the river at no charge. He gladly agreed to take her across, but stipulated that she would have to go to bed with him first. She refused and headed back home.*
>
> *On her way home, she ran into her friend Ivan. She explained her situation and Sinbad's offer. She asked if he could help her in some way.*
>
> *"You know," said Ivan, "This sounds kind of messy, I don't think I want to get involved in this. Besides, I'm in a hurry. I'm sorry," he said and walked away.*
>
> *Abigail, feeling totally hopeless and at the mercy of the situation, went back to Sinbad, consented, and traveled across the river. Once she was on the other side, she tearfully explained to Gregory all that she had gone through to be with him.*
>
> *Gregory was livid! He could not believe what she had done. He insisted that she leave immediately.*
>
> *Dejected, hurt, and angry, Abigail went into town and ran into a fellow named Sludge. She explained to him the whole sordid story. Upon hearing this, Sludge became angry. He found Gregory and demanded that he apologize to Abigail and take her back. When Gregory refused, Sludge became even more angry and beat him up. Abigail laughed.*

And the winner is...

I'd like for you to take a moment to think about the characters in the story and *rank* them in terms of whom you found to be the most offensive. Using a scale of 1–5, number 1 would be the least offensive character and number 5 the most offensive. Each character can only be assigned one number from the scale. **(Illustration 4.1)**

Illustration 4.1 | The Story of Abigail and Sinbad

Illustration

Character	Most Offensive				Least Offensive
Abigail	5	4	3	2	1
Gregory	5	4	3	2	1
Sinbad	5	4	3	2	1
Ivan	5	4	3	2	1
Sludge	5	4	3	2	1

It would really be helpful if you could find a friend to read the story and rank the characters according to how they see them and then compare responses. I think you'll be very surprised at how differently people see and feel about the characters in the story.

I've worked with people who see Abigail as the most offensive character because she manipulated Sludge into beating up Gregory. Others ranked her as most offensive because she laughed. Still others see Abigail as the least offensive. She was a victim having made the "supreme sacrifice."

Some people see Ivan as a neutral character and others see him as offensive because he refused to help in this situation.

People's views differ greatly in terms of how they make these decisions.

If you are expecting a "right" answer, I'm sorry, there is none. The way you ranked the characters is a reflection of your values and judgments, your feelings and emotions and the rational, objective part of you.

People make decisions based on these three criteria all the time. Problems arise because they make an emotional decision when an objective decision would be more appropriate, or they're making an objective decision that is tainted by values or emotions that are inappropriate for the situation.

It's important that we understand these three criteria because they drive our behavior and the behavior of others. Let's take a look.

Know thyself

Back in the 1950s Dr. Eric Berne developed a behavioral model called Transactional Analysis. This model identifies three functional parts of our personality. He called them Ego States and named them Parent, Adult, and Child. These are the aforementioned criteria: your values and judgments (Parent), your feelings and emotions (Child), and the rational, objective part of you (Adult).

Human behavior is extraordinarily complex and cannot be conveniently explained away with this model, and yet I've used this model with thousands of people over the years. The reason that I find it so valuable is because it gives us insight into the behavior of others, which clues us into how we need to manage ourselves, especially in difficult situations. Most importantly, it provides insight into why we behave as we do. It also gives us language with which to describe that behavior. Such knowledge and insight doesn't always keep one out of trouble. At any given moment we can say and do things of which we are less than proud. But you can look back on those situations, analyze them, and decide how you might respond differently to achieve a different result. The next time you face similar circumstances, you will likely avoid trouble by responding more appropriately.

I invite you to take the *Understanding Self and Others* questionnaire on my website if you would like more information on how much of your personality is invested in the three Ego States. **www.readysetgrow.biz**.

Let's begin with an understanding of the three Ego States. **(Illustration 4.2)**

Illustration 4.2 | The Three Ego States

Illustration

Child, Parent, Adult Ego States

The Child. The Child Ego State is the emotional part of us. It's what we come into the world with. It is here that all of our natural urges, feelings, and desires are stored.

The way a baby experiences his world has a profound impact on how he feels about himself and others once he becomes an adult. When a child makes his needs known and those needs are met, he feels good about himself and the world around him.

Children who are ignored or abused do not feel good about themselves or the people around them. They are likely to grow up with low self-esteem and an inability to trust others.

Most of us are unable to remember our first few years of life but everything that happens to us is recorded in the brain. It's not always easy to access that information, but it is in there. It has made an impression: sometimes a good impression and sometimes impressions that bruise our personality.

The Parent. The next Ego State to develop is the Parent. This is where all our judgments, perceptual styles, values, and teachings are stored. We see this developing very clearly in children aged 18–24 months. Watch a toddler when they are with younger children. They attempt to parent these babies with instructions like, No! Sit down! Don't touch that! These children are simply playing back what they've heard their parents say to them.

Toddlers have moved from a stage of total dependence to one of interdependence. They are extremely curious and creative. Left to their own devices, they would explore their environment and most assuredly injure themselves. As a result, parents watch them carefully and repeatedly say the words "ought," "always," "never," and "should." As children get older, parental messages continue to be stored in the Parent.

Now, as an adult, you know why you find yourself repeating to your children the same things that drove you crazy when you were a kid.

The Parent Ego State is not unlike a computer — garbage in, garbage out. Contaminated data such as negative stereotypes, prejudices and experiences can be stored at a very early age and result in unhealthy ways of looking at the world.

My sister-in-law serves her community as a Big Sister. I was in her city visiting for a few days when I met her "Little Sister." She asked me a few harmless questions about my husband, Richard, who was not on the trip. Then she calmly asked, "what if he's been cheating on you while you were away?" I explained that my husband is not that kind of man. This seven-year-old coolly informed me, "all men cheat." Unfortunately, this little girl has had very limited and negative exposure to men and she's generalized her experience as common to all. It now resides in the Parent part of her personality.

The Adult. The Adult Ego State is the rational, problem-solving part of the personality. This Ego State is fully developed about the age of 12 when, as Swiss child psychologist Jean Piaget tells us, the brain has changed and young people are now able to think conceptually. The Adult Ego State functions to analyze data that is stored in the Parent and in the Child. It performs a few reality checks and updates that information. If you have been raised with negative stereotypes such as *"a woman's place is in the kitchen and the bedroom"* but you've had the opportunity to partner with women in the workplace, your Adult thinking would challenge that early teaching, reject it, and make a more informed decision.

We need all three Ego States, the Parent, the Adult, and the Child, to live as a fully functioning person. One is no better than the other, although in the workplace, you will need to spend more time in the Adult Ego State.

Free Child and Adapted Child

The Child Ego State can be divided into two major areas, the Adapted Child and the Free Child (**Illustration 4.3**).

Illustration

Illustration 4.3 | The Child Ego State

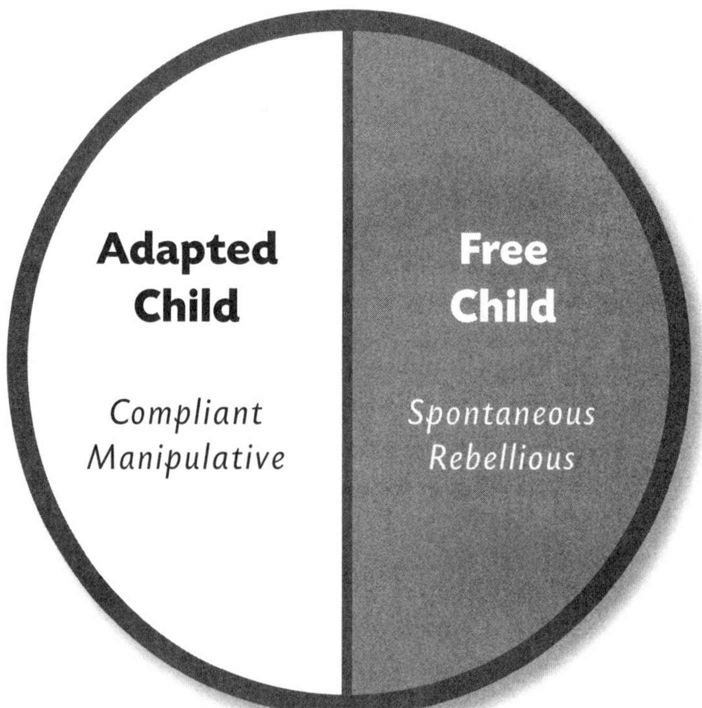

The Free Child is the fun-loving, spontaneous part of the Child personality. You'll know it by the laughter, spontaneity, and animated behavior. This type of behavior is very appropriate and very positive at parties, sporting events, with family, and on some social occasions. It's less appropriate in work meetings when problem-solving and business needs are discussed.

The Free Child is also the rebellious part of the personality. It's what's operating when someone cuts you off in traffic. When choice words are exchanged and both parties spring from their vehicles ready for an altercation, that's Free Child behavior. It's when you're not considering the situation and consequences, but reacting in anger to not getting your way.

The Adapted Child is that part of a child's personality that parents, educators, and older siblings try to shape and mold so children can get along in society. Children must learn to walk into rooms and say, "Excuse me, Mommy, may I have a cookie, please?" The child's natural impulse is to run through the house and grab the cookies off the table without asking anyone's permission. They have to learn to sublimate those Free Child urges and desires and behave in a way that's acceptable in our society.

Adapted Child behavior is the manipulative part of the Child personality. I'm sure most of you know situations where young children appear to be running the household. These young people have figured out Mom's and Dad's "hot" buttons and hold them hostage to their wants and desires. These kids are master manipulators. Everything revolves around them and around making them happy… or at least keeping them quiet.

Adapted Child behavior is unfortunately not limited to children. Have you ever seen an adult throw a temper tantrum or con and manipulate others to get their way? In organizations, these are "Yes" persons. When they're with one group they are agreeing with them. When they're with another group, they'll agree with them. They sway with the wind, walk the fence; they go along to get along. They stand for nothing and can only be trusted to do what is in their best interest.

Nurturing Parent and Critical Parent

There are two major areas of the Parent: the Nurturing Parent and the Critical Parent. Look at **Illustration 4.4**:

Illustration

Illustration 4.4 | The Parent Ego State

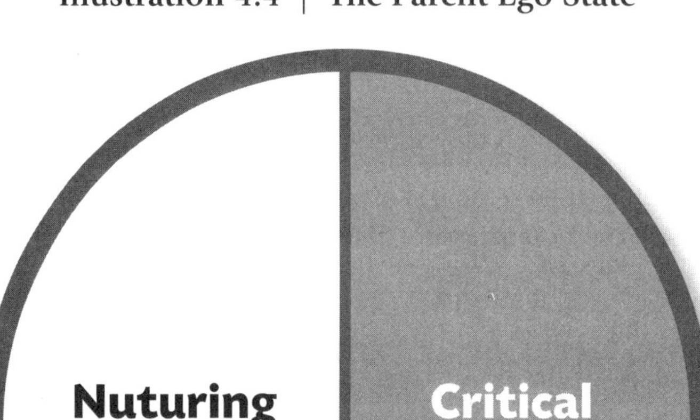

The Nurturing Parent is the part of the Parent personality that is kind, warm, affirming, loving, and validating. It's the come-to-Mommy-let-me-kiss-it-and-make-it-all-better type of behavior. There are times in the workplace when a supportive arm on the shoulder, or sharing a cup of coffee to see how you're doing, is very reassuring. People are constantly challenged with life-changing events, personal and professional losses, and the normal vicissitudes of life.

Whenever I work with leaders who have a team that loves them, are willing to build brick walls, walk through them and then build them again — those leaders have strong Nurturing Parent behavior. Their people are willing to work through the weekend without a shower or change of clothes because they want to please their leader. (I may be overstating that just a bit.) The point is that they will do whatever is necessary because they believe that leader cares about them and that makes them feel important.

Nurturing Parent behavior takes a turn for the worse when it becomes overbearing and stifling because it doesn't allow people to grow. For example, if you worked for someone with an uncontained Nurturing Parent and you said to him or her, in a whining voice, "I'm not sure I can get this project completed on time in addition to my normal work." What is unsaid but clearly heard is "help me, I can't do this." This Nurturing Parent would respond, "Well Dearie, don't you worry about it. Just go on home. I'll take care of it for you." This is a lose-lose situation. The manager is overloaded with work and the subordinate doesn't face up to responsibility.

The other side of the Nurturing Parent is the Critical Parent. This is the "How-many-times-do-I-have-to-tell-you-how-to-do-this? You-should-know-this-by-now," type of behavior.

There *are* times when people need a swift kick to get them going. However, you can only do that to the extent that you care for them and have affirmed them. Critical Parent is a style that people really, really dislike. This style may initially get results, but the long-term results are poor. Leaders with high Critical Parent behavior are not able to keep or attract people, or to get staff members working at their highest level of performance.

Adult functioning

The Adult functions to determine when it's appropriate to go into the various Ego States.

In the workplace, it's most important that you operate from the Adult behavior style. The Adult should be the executor or executrix of your personality. You will occasionally spend time in Child or Parent behavior, but let the Adult decide when that's appropriate.

> *Some years ago, I had a client whose Child was the executor of his personality. Josh was a very successful attorney specializing in Real Estate law. His wife was a teacher and they had two beautiful daughters. Together, they enjoyed a very good income. He and his family lived in a two-bedroom apartment in Manhattan, which he rented. One could not help but wonder why someone at his income level, with a family, would rent. It was perplexing. When probed on this, he confessed that he was afraid to take on long-term debt.*

When Josh was a young boy, his father passed away suddenly and left the family penniless. He was the oldest of four children and closest to his mother's struggles to get food on the table. In his 10-year-old mind "gloom and doom was just around the corner"... *and it was.*

The scared 10-year-old part of his personality never left him. In fact, it became the executor of his personality. Thirty years later, in spite of dramatically different financial circumstances, Josh would not take out a loan because he still believed "gloom and doom was just around the corner."

Had the Adult been functioning and critically examining this belief, he would have determined the following: He had a very good job; his wife had a good job; and together, they made more than enough to handle a mortgage. The decision was made from the Child and was irrational.

Who is the executor of your personality? Let's interpret your results from the online questionnaire.

Reviewing the graph

If you have not taken the online questionnaire, you can skip this next section and continue reading at Helpful Hints on page 88.

Illustration 4.5 | Pat Perfect

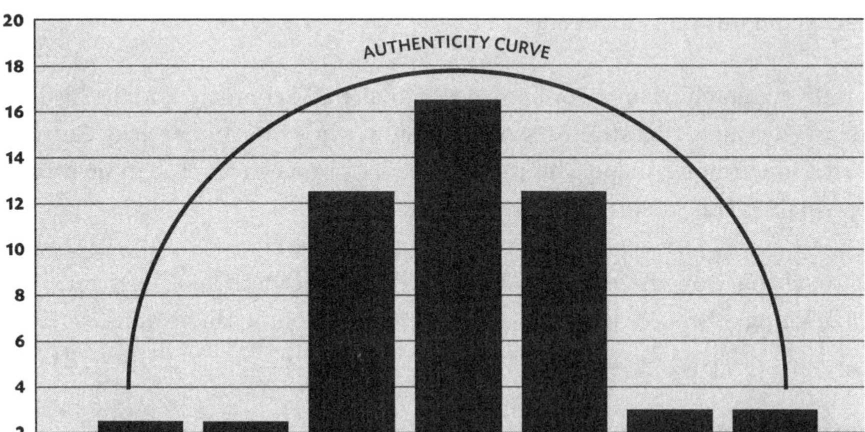

Illustration

I prefer to interpret the graph **(Illustration 4.5)** by first identifying the healthy positions of Nurturing Parent, Adult, and Free Child. I like to see those scores at "8" or higher.

- ☛ If your Free Child score is below "8," you are probably not having enough fun.
- ☛ If your Nurturing Parent score is below "8," you have an opportunity to impact people in a more positive way.
- ☛ If your Adult score is below "8," you may be experiencing life's circumstances managing you as opposed to your managing them.
- ☛ If your Critical Parent, Rescuing Parent, Helpless Child or Defensive Child is over "8," put a check next to it. We will return to it later.

I have not described Rebellious Child and Helpless Child behaviors because I think they are self-explanatory.

The Rescuing Parent is an extreme version of Nurturing Parent. This is the father who continually bails out his son and gets him out of scraps as opposed to just letting the boy spend a night in jail so he can learn a lesson. Sometimes parents don't want their children to hurt so they rescue them. But when children never experience the consequences of their decisions and behavior, they don't mature properly and this hurts them later.

Look at your graph from the online questionnaire and compare it to the healthy Authenticity Curve **(Illustration 4.5)**. You can see how the Authenticity Curve is arcing in a concave shape. This perfect person is one I have yet to meet. Most people have graphs that look like roller coasters.

You can change your graph and your life by reducing certain Ego States and strengthening others. It takes time and a lot of work, but it can be done.

Helpful hints

Review the Helpful Hints **(Illustration 4.6)** to learn how you can decrease or increase the Ego State requiring attention. I suggest you focus on no more than two Ego States.

Illustration

Illustration 4.6 | Helpful Hints

To increase my Nurturing Parent

1. Openly express your concern and care for others.
2. Be sure to comment on all the good points you can find in others. Tell your family you love them.
3. Give recognition to others freely. Don't wait till they "do" something.
4. Listen intently to what others are saying.

To increase Adult Awareness

1. Describe the state of your body in terms of sensations, soreness, and temperature starting with your toes and going to your head.
2. Concentrate intensely as you talk to another person. Listen carefully to what is being said by both of you.
3. Do some sort of physical exercise until you are aware of your body and your internal sensations.

To increase Adult Objectivity

1. Make a list of top priority values for your life.
2. Make a list of specific plans for goals you want to accomplish.
3. Organize each day so that you know where you are going and what you are to accomplish.

To increase Authenticity

1. Be willing to share a friendship at every opportunity.
2. Decide that you will be yourself instead of what you think others expect you to be.
3. Avoid all forms of criticism, ridicule or persecution.
4. Do not offer advice unless specifically asked.
5. Look for opportunities to praise and express your good feelings toward others.

To increase my Free Child

1. Schedule time to enjoy yourself
2. Establish hobbies and enjoyable times with friends and family.
3. Decide that worrying will not change your situation. Instead, look for positive ways to solve your problems.
4. Think of something to say or do that will make the kid inside of you laugh and giggle. Sing, whistle or hum as loudly as possible.
5. Stop rehearsing what you are going to say to others.

To decrease my Critical Parent (see Helpless Child)

1. Stop expecting perfection. Stop saying "should," "ought," etc.
2. Attack problems – not people. Be willing to live with "practical" solutions.
3. Listen intently to the whole story before making judgment; thoroughly examine both sides of problems – yours and theirs.
4. Examine and avoid all negative or critical opinions; listen to yourself.
5. Be nice to yourself. Plan ahead for time to play.

To decrease my Rescuing Parent

1. Do not offer advice unless you are asked.
2. Get in touch with your guilt and how it motivates your behavior.
3. Insist that people ask for what they want – refuse to think or answer for others.
4. Love people for themselves, not their weakness or dependency.

To decrease my Helpless Child

1. Say "Yes" or "No" without explaining.
2. Stop saying "I can't"; say "I won't" instead.
3. Set short-range goals and compliment yourself for small accomplishments.
4. Recognize that you have the power to cause change. Ask for what you want and expect to receive it.
5. Make things happen.

To decrease my Defensive Child (see Rescuing Parent)

1. Refuse to argue about your decisions.
2. Get rid of your angry or negative feelings. Pray or think about forgiveness, even if at first you are not sincere.
3. Openly admit your anger, failures, mistakes and shortcomings. Accept the responsibilitiy for your own destiny.
4. Commit to and follow through on a goals program.

Now take those suggestions and write them on a 3 x 5 card or input them into your handheld PDA. Make sure they are somewhere you will see them every day. Read it daily, and in time you will begin to internalize them. Initially, you may become aware after the fact of when and how you've engaged in not-okay behavior. In a bit more time, you may become more aware in the moment and then, in perhaps in six months or so, you're going to avoid inappropriate behavior altogether.

You've probably identified situations where you would have been more effective had you used Adult behavior as opposed to another behavior that is more comfortable for you. You may also be thinking how difficult it must be to modify your behavior in this way. You're right. It is difficult, but not impossible. And the rewards are worth the effort. I assure you, it will work if you work it.

I recently worked with a woman who was very bright, talented, and industrious. She could outproduce all her counterparts and, as a result, became a valuable resource on her team. When she took the self-reflection instrument, we observed significant Rescuing Parent and Helpless Child behavior.

This woman would not say no to the requests of others. She became overburdened, and, as a result, deadlines would slip. Over the next several months, she worked on strengthening her ability to say no and manage a reasonable workload by increasing her Adult behavior. She did it! Several months later, she redid the instrument and her results were dramatic and positive. She has since been promoted and is currently on a very strong and positive career track.

Between me and thee

What happens in your work environment between and among team members when each member of your team exhibits behavior that is unique to them because of the differences in Parent, Adult, and Child Ego States? Some may be more controlling and directive (Parent), others passive and adaptive (Child) and still others thoughtful and reflective (Adult). Since we need to get along with everyone, it's important to understand the three types of interpersonal exchanges (transactions) that can occur.

Complimentary transactions

Complimentary transactions involve expected responses. Here is an example:

VJH: "What time is it?"
Colleague: "It's three o'clock."

This was a complimentary, Adult-to-Adult transaction. (See **Illustration 4.7 — diagram A** on page 92) I was hoping to hook a particular Ego State and I did. I got the expected response.

My friend, Jackie, called me from L.A. after the Yankees won the World Series. I picked up the phone and heard:
Jackie: "AWESOME! I can't believe it! They did it again!
VJH: "We're number one!"

This Child-to-Child transaction is also complimentary.
(See **Illustration 4.7 — diagram B**)

A complimentary Parent-to-Parent transaction would sound something like this:

"Isn't it awful about the reorganization?"
"Here we go again; we just reorganized six months ago!"
"The people at the top just don't know what the heck they're doing."
"I know, and the worst of it is they make all the money and we do all the work!"

Sound familiar?

The two parties involved are both speaking from their Critical Parent (see **Illustration 4.7 — diagram C**), blaming and putting down a third party. They are unconsciously giving each other strokes and recognition for being better, stronger, and smarter than the parties they are complaining about. It's a fun game because the participants feel so powerful and superior. But it's a counterfeit game. Lacking in authenticity, these kinds of games don't fully satisfy our need for stroking and recognition. As a result, participants must continue to play the game. After all, counterfeit strokes are better than no strokes at all.

Illustration

Illustration 4.7 | Complimentary Transactions

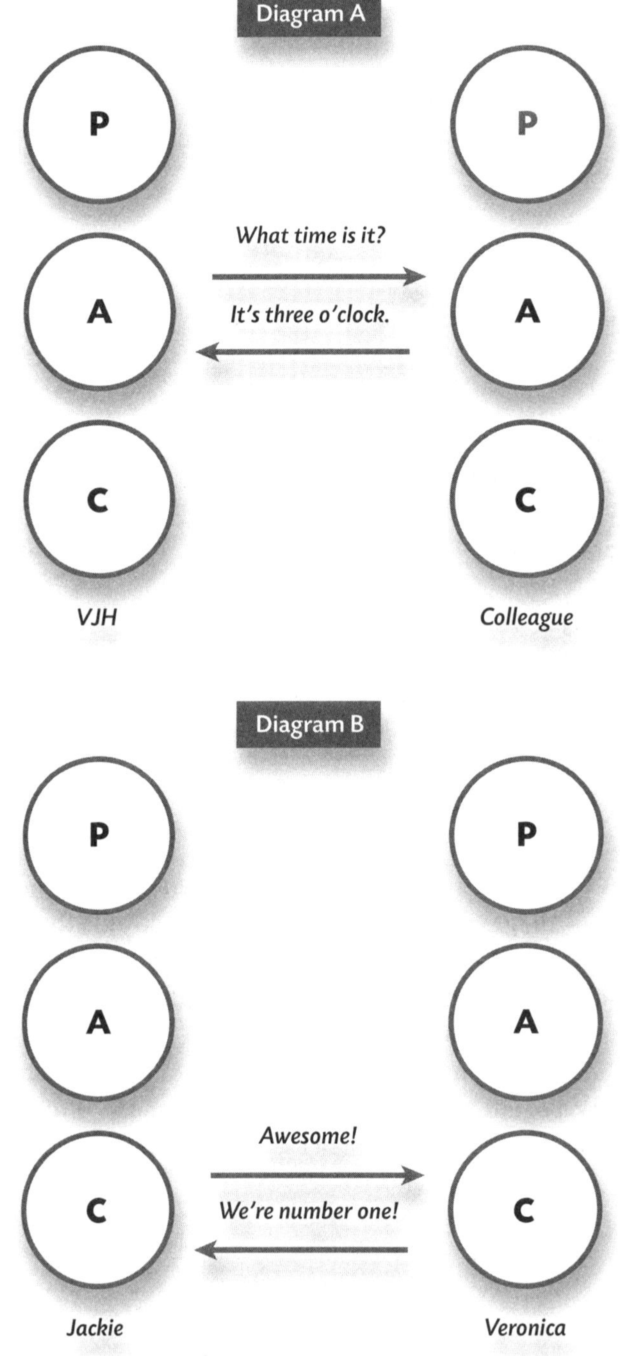

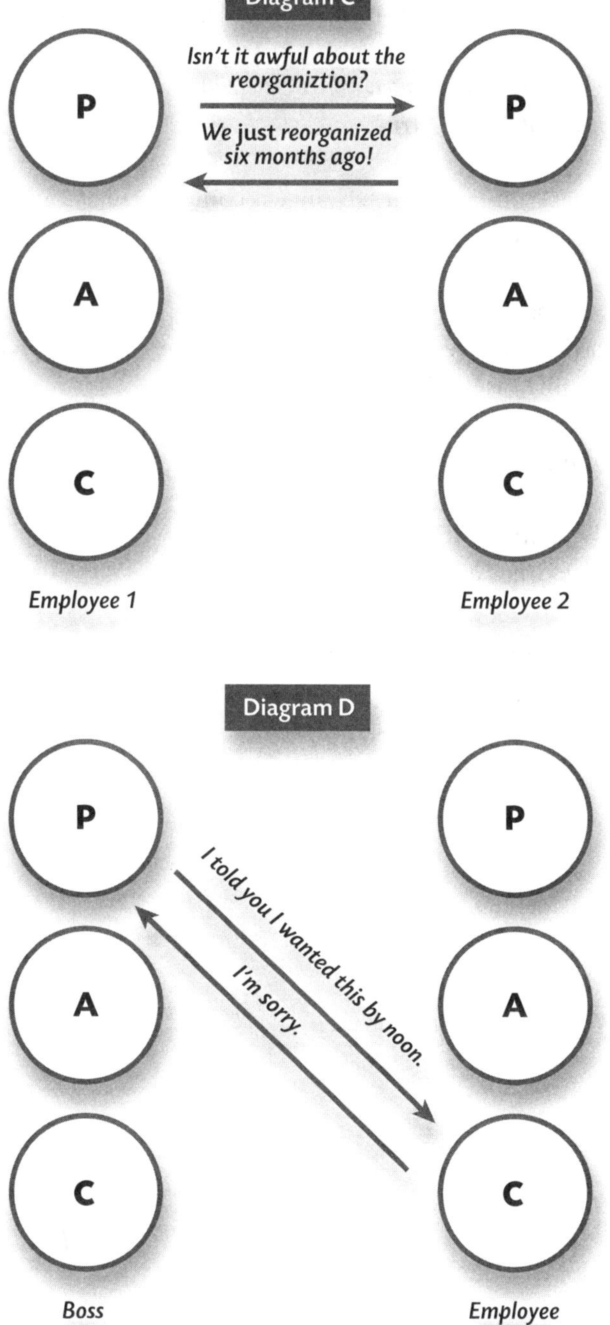
Diagram C
Isn't it awful about the reorganiztion?
We just reorganized six months ago!
P
P
A
A
C
C
Employee 1
Employee 2
Diagram D
P
P
I told you I wanted this by noon.
I'm sorry.
A
A
C
C
Boss
Employee

When the workplace is devoid of recognition and stroking, people will fill up their time with this kind of counterproductive game playing.

Just because a transaction is a complimentary does not mean that it is positive. Consider this example (See **Illustration 4.7 — diagram D** on page 93):

Boss: "I thought I told you I wanted this completed by noon."
Employee: (sheepishly) "I'm sorry."

A Parent-to-Child, Child-to-Parent exchange is complimentary but in the case of this boss and employee inappropriate and unproductive.

Crossed transactions

A crossed transaction involves an unexpected response, crossed signals. It sounds negative, and in some cases it is.

Consider this example:

Mary Ann: "What time is it?"
VJH: "Mary Ann, when are you going to buy a watch?"

Mary Ann was expecting Adult behavior, but received an unexpected Critical Parent response from me. (See **Illustration 4.8 — diagram A** on the next page)

Illustration

Illustration 4.8 | Crossed Transactions

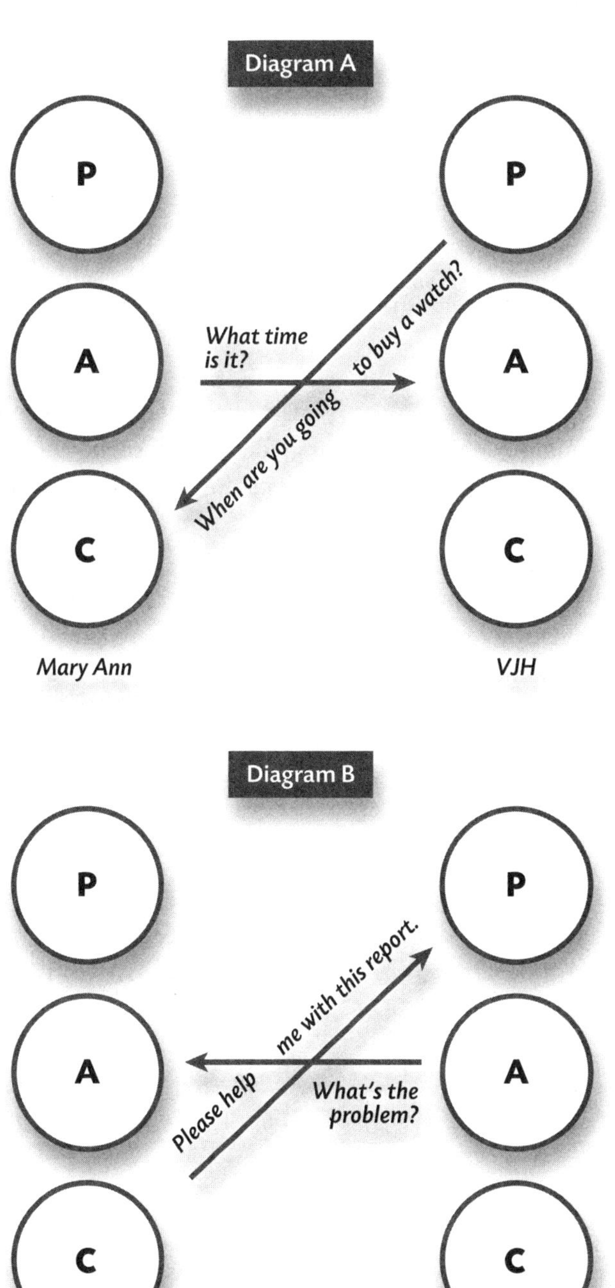

When the transaction is crossed, the *communication* stops, even though the *conversation* continues.

Mary Ann: "My goodness! What side of the bed did you get up on today?"
VJH: "That's none of your business."

We're off to a pretty heated exchange.

Obviously, crossed transactions can have a negative impact. If you're involved in a conversation and it stops abruptly, with you left feeling uncomfortable, it's very likely that a crossed transaction has just occurred. For example, you're in a meeting and updating team members on a project you've been working on. In the middle of your explanation, the meeting facilitator interrupts and says with a curt tone, "Didn't we hear this information at the last meeting?" Regardless of the answer, this crossed transaction can result in you feeling deflated and humiliated. (Same as **Illustration 4.8 — diagram A**)

Believe it or not, crossed transactions can be healthy and productive. Knowing when and how to use them is an important skill to learn, particularly in the situation I'm about to describe.

Subordinate: "Gee, Veronica, I'm really, really struggling. I've been trying to work with this particular software to produce the quarterly reports and, for the life of me, I can't figure it out."

This employee is coming to me from his Helpless Child trying to "hook" my Rescuing Parent so I can relieve him of the project. Since I want to have an Adult-to-Adult conversation and relationship with this individual, my response is to cross the transaction with:

VJH: "Tell me more about what you're struggling with," or "Help me understand where the difficulties are," or "What are you having specific problems with?"

I crossed the transaction by asking an Adult question. **(Illustration 4.8 — diagram B)**

When you ask an Adult question, people — regardless of whether they're coming from their Parent or Child — have to stop, think and then respond. My strategy is to cause them to respond from their Adult and elevate the conversation to an Adult-to-Adult level. If I acknowledge and respond to the Helpless Child, I will likely get more Helpless Child behavior.

Sometimes when people come to us from their Helpless Child, we respond from our Critical Parent out of habit and frustration. Since *what we stroke is what we get,* we are conditioning this person to give us more of what we find so frustrating. We can help them to think from their Adult simply by asking Adult questions. There is no guarantee that they will, but no matter what they do or don't do, you can protect yourself by remaining Adult, professional, calm, cool and collected in the situation.

This is a very important skill to learn. In fact it is the most important thing of all that we've talked about in this chapter. Your ability to get along with difficult people depends on your being able to:

- ☛ Understand where people are coming from in terms of Parent, Adult, and Child behaviors
- ☛ Respond from your Adult when appropriate
- ☛ Ask questions

Helpful Hint: The person asking the questions controls the conversation.

Not long ago, I was visiting with the Human Resources Professional at a client firm. There had been reorganization and she was dealing with multiple people issues. It was not unusual for her to be ensconced in closed-door meetings much of the day and then in the office late at night working.

As she talked, I suspected that part of her problem was that she was responding to individuals from her Rescuing Parent. She had unwittingly been sucked into a game with "Poor Me" players. Her role in the game was to offer suggestions they didn't really want, rather than help them manage their problems themselves. While they came with the problems, she unknowingly paid the bill.

The Understanding Self and Others questionnaire confirmed her high Rescuing Parent and she enthusiastically started to apply the Helpful Hints to reduce it. When I checked in with her about six weeks later, she proudly shared that she had not had one closed-door meeting since our conversation and she was getting home on time.

She had learned not to take the bait.

Ulterior transactions

The third type of transaction is called an Ulterior Transaction. There are two levels to this transaction, the surface level and the ulterior or psychological level.

It's at the ulterior level that the true meaning of the transaction lives.

For example, if an employee comes to work late and her boss says,

Boss: "What time is it, Debbie?" (Surface level)

What is the boss really saying? Well, it's loud and clear...

Boss: "You're late." (Ulterior level)

Again, there are some conversations where the words say one thing but you're feeling something else. The true meaning is at that ulterior, psychological level. **(Illustration 4.9)**

Illustration

Illustration 4.9 | Ulterior Transactions

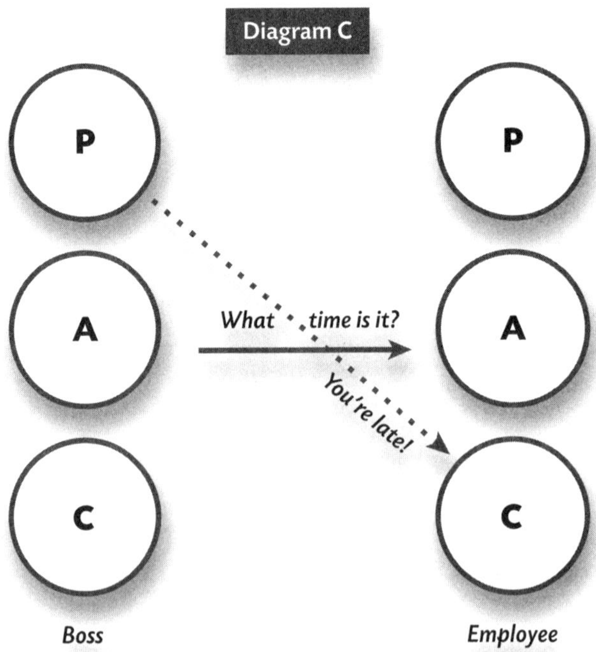

Protect yourself

You can also use this information to help protect yourself from getting emotionally hooked and accepting bad feelings from others. You *don't* have to receive bad feelings from anyone! Your boss or colleague may come at you with Critical Parent behavior, but that doesn't mean *you* have to go into Helpless Child mode. Stay in your Adult and ask questions, ask questions, ask questions. Ask questions such as…tell me more about that…are you saying that...?, do you mean...?, help me understand…?

> *Many years ago, I disappointed a superior with a project I submitted to him for review. Disappointed is an understatement. Actually, he was livid and blew his top in front of the entire office. He demanded to know who had written the document. I had not written it independently and I did not want to take full responsibility for its outcome. From my Adult, I asked if he made specific comments about what he would prefer to see, when could I get this is back to him, etc. By the time I took the elevator up one floor and returned to my desk, he had called my boss to apologize. You see, his behavior caused him to look like a jerk while I remained, at least on the outside, cool, calm and collected.*

Caution

The information in this chapter has not been presented to be used against others. Use it to help you analyze and evaluate *your* responses only. It would be unwise to label and pigeonhole people you work with because you think you've got the goods on them. And, never, ever go to someone and say, "Ha! I think that's Parent behavior." They will not appreciate it.

Action plan

I'd like you to think about the situations and people that give you the most difficulty. Under what circumstances do you find your Rescuing Parent, Helpless Child, or Critical Parent being hooked inappropriately? Jot those down in **Success Step 4.1** on the next page.

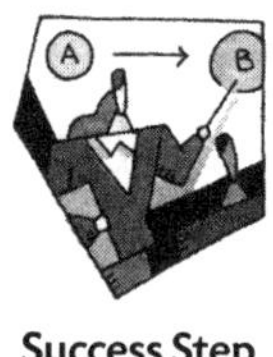

Success Step

Success Step 4.1

1.	
2.	
3.	
4.	
5.	
6.	
7.	

Now diagram a typical scenario. What is said to you and how do you respond?

Illustration

Illustration 4.10

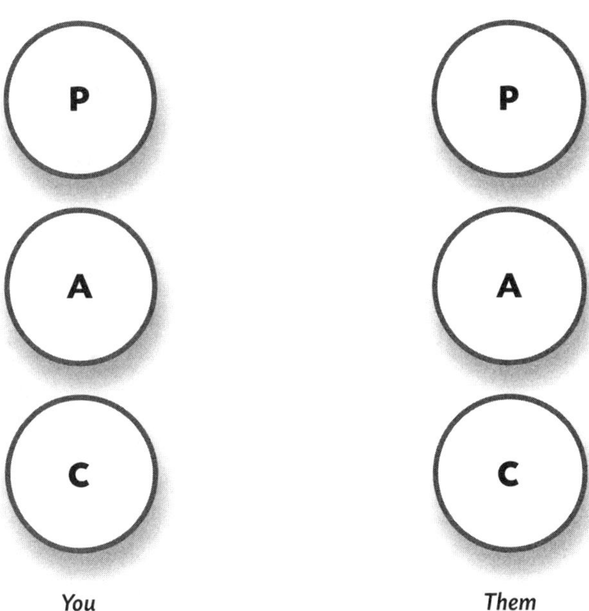

Now rewrite the script. Jot down what is typically said to you and how you will respond from your Adult behavior style to the other person.

Make copies and use these worksheets whenever you find yourself slipping into negative behavior.

Remember: *The system will work if you work the system!*

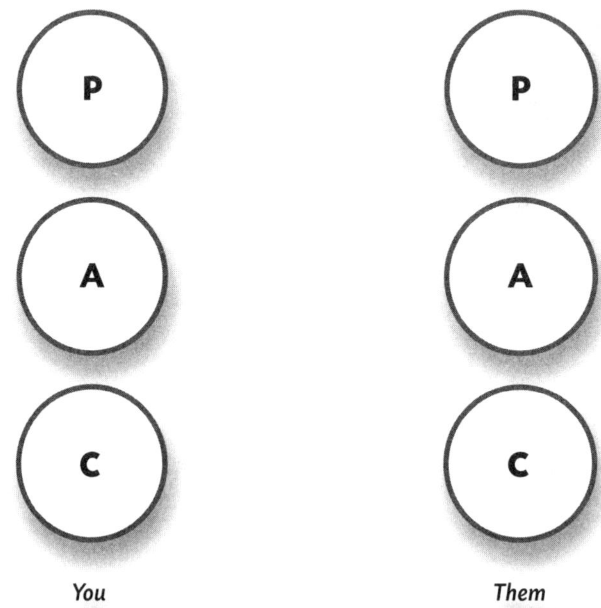

CHAPTER 5
Developing Executive Presence

Not long ago, I was speaking with a former client who has been unable to retire because a suitable replacement has not been found. Though his organization has interviewed some very strong, talented, and skillful candidates, they have held back on making an offer because all the candidates lacked Executive Presence.

What is Executive Presence?

We hear this term bandied around quite a bit and perhaps we know it when we see it, but just what is it?

Executive Presence is an impression, an image, an aura, a type of charisma or magnetism. It's a presence that speaks without words, a quality that is attractive to people and that attracts people. Gill Scott, former executive with Xerox, describes it as "The Leadership Mantle," it's a part of who you are. He believes you are either born with it or not.

It may sound a bit shallow for an organization to be so concerned with an individual's outer self. And I would agree — if that were all they considered. But remember that it's not just *what* you do but *how* you do it. And the way you carry yourself is of major importance. Organizations are made up of people and, like it or not, people make judgments about others based on physical impressions. We all do.

I'll prove it to you.

If you had a choice to ask directions of a person dressed in business attire or someone who appeared to be homeless, whom would you ask?

Or, imagine that the next time you boarded an airplane you noticed the crew was out of uniform and dressed in street clothes. How would you feel? Comfortable? I think not. Does what the crew is wearing have anything to do with their ability to operate the aircraft? Of course not. But it does affect our perception of their abilities.

Have you ever seen a military briefing on television where the top brass does *not* have on its uniforms with medals and stripes in full view? Not likely.

We have an expectation and a need to see an airline crew, our military leaders, and our workplace leaders in their proper attire. It gives us a sense of security.

Executive Presence is more than clothing. It's an inner quality as well. Who would you prefer to follow into battle, Colin Powell or Woody Allen? I happen to think that Woody Allen is a very intelligent and talented man, but Colin Powell exudes a physical and mental strength, a confidence and self-assuredness, that makes him the leader I would follow into battle.

People in leadership are expected to dress and carry themselves in a way that befits their position. It doesn't matter if you're an aspiring leader or not. If you wish to increase your influence and your impact within your organization, paying attention to your image is crucial. Fortunately, Executive Presence *can* be developed.

Why is Executive Presence important?

Over the course of 20 years, I have coached many talented and competent professionals whose careers have been called into question because they lacked Executive Presence.

John is an extraordinary talent, but top management at his firm does not perceive him as "executive material." John is as intelligent, perhaps even more so, as anyone on the executive team. Yet his body language, dress, tone, lack of participation, and tentative attitude communicate that he is less than confident and secure. The team does not perceive him as "one of the boys" or someone possessing leadership potential.

As part of a plan to help John see what others were seeing about him, we videotaped him and critiqued his behavior. John could see that during a particularly important and stressful meeting, he unconsciously ran his fingers through his hair so often that he looked like he had just gotten out of bed. His belt was not securely held through all the loops and his shirttail was not properly tucked into his pants. John didn't sit erect in his chair, his shoulders were rounded and slumped. He held his face in the cup of his hands with his elbows on the table. As if that weren't bad enough, he had a nervous twitch and constantly shook his leg. He doodled on his pad while other executives appeared to be engaged in the discussion and poised to attack the issue at hand. John did not step up to the plate by providing direction or adding value to the meeting.

John was shocked and dismayed by what he saw on the video. He then excused himself, went into the men's room, adjusted his clothing and combed his hair. We role played a few situations and forced him to sit up straight and speak with poised dignity. The difference was also pretty amazing. John learned that he needed to become more conscious of his behavior.

I recommended that John work with an image consultant and a personal trainer. He agreed. His work with the trainer caused him to become more aware of healthy eating habits (Twinkies had been his lunch of choice) and the need to improve his body image. My objective was less about him "beefing up" and more about developing the type of confidence that comes from within when you are in good physical condition.

The image consultant took John shopping and helped him purchase a wardrobe that worked with his physique, skin tone, and budget. After following her advice for new glasses and a new haircut, John has improved his look considerably. I'm very proud of him. And I believe that the subsequent feedback he has received on his sharper appearance and newfound confidence has helped him feel better about himself and stay on the straight and narrow. I've occasionally been in his office just as John was returning from a meeting. And I'm happy to report that the disaster of an image he used to possess is now long gone.

People want their leaders and executives to look *and* act the part. When your image fails you, others will filter what you say through their perception of how they think you *should* look and act. If people don't like what they see, it's very hard for them to hear what you have to say. As a result, your good ideas and insights can fall on deaf ears and limit your impact, no matter how strong your skills and talents are.

> *Sarah is a young woman who started her career in a support role. She is very bright and demonstrates insight and intelligence beyond her years and position. Though her work is exemplary and far beyond her level, her appearance and dress are not. In a crowded room most people would automatically perceive her as a junior person. Frankly, she lacks polish. Her clothes fit poorly and are obviously inexpensive. Sarah tends to wear trendy clothing that is completely unflattering on a full-figured body. She often arrives at work with damp hair. As a result, her manager is hesitant to put her in front of clients or senior people in the organization.*

Enjoying a well cooked meal is part presentation; good work must also be packaged and delivered in a way that is appropriate, exciting, and comfortable for others. In Sarah's case, her stellar performance was not enough. She needed to take time and focus on the package. Your clothes need to be appropriate for your organization and the level you aspire to and, regardless of your weight, they should fit well. That means if you're dieting and you have a significant amount of weight to lose, don't wait until you reach your goal. You may need to purchase additional clothing as you're losing weight to ensure a well pulled together look. A strong appearance is achievable and desirable for anyone regardless of gender, weight, or budget.

Dressing for success

We must put our best foot forward whenever we present ourselves to people. I would lose all credibility if I attempted to give a work-related presentation in jeans and a sweatshirt. People don't expect to see that kind of dress from a presenter in a workplace situation. They'd have no problem with it if they were visiting my home on a Saturday afternoon. But in a business context, they would have difficulty hearing me because they'd be confused as to why I was dressed that way.

Clothing not only makes a difference in your outer appearance, it impacts your inner self as well. Wearing clothes that make you feel attractive gives you a sense of security. Walking into a room knowing that you look good and that you fit in gives you a sense of confidence and comfort that others easily pick up on.

Strengthening your image can go a long way to increasing your ability to be heard. I recently worked with a woman who holds a Ph.D. from an Ivy League university and a very responsible position in a *Fortune* 100 company.

Despite her academic and industry success, Anne was not very confident. Part of the problem was her language. She was born and raised outside the United States and had a very strong accent. As a result, she could be difficult to understand. Feeling insecure about this, she tended to be quiet in meetings and did not ask enough questions when given assignments. She also focused on the tasks at hand and spent no time developing important relationships. Anne felt like an outsider in the workplace and her wardrobe reflected this lack of self-esteem. In spite of her healthy salary, her clothing was clearly purchased at "popularly priced" stores and they generally lacked color and style. While there was nothing wrong with what she wore, her clothes did not bespeak her position and education. Other women at her level wore classic, conservative, and quietly expensive clothing. Anne could afford to present herself better, but she never saw it as important. At the same time, she continually struggled to gain influence in the organization.

Powerful people tend to take up more space, so smaller women or men can have an inherent disadvantage. Anne was a petite, soft-spoken woman. We wanted to create a more powerful perception of her. This required her to appear to take up more space. We brought out the video camera and worked on her vocal projection and body language. She needed to speak louder and use gestures more strategically. We also worked on her presentation skills so she would have a more powerful delivery style. We developed strategies (conversation starters, ways to transition in and out of conversations, listening) that allowed her to take advantage of social time before and after meetings to strengthen relationships within and outside her group. Anne also had a total makeover including makeup and clothing. She has become a stunning woman. You can't walk into a room and not see and *feel her presence.*

Your image may have to extend beyond your clothing. Depending on your occupation you may need to drive a certain type of car, live in a certain type of home, play golf, and belong to certain types of clubs or organizations. Doctors, lawyers, and executives often need to demonstrate their success through these outward appearances. It lets the rest of us believe, rightly or wrongly, that because they have a measure of success, they can be trusted to handle our legal, financial, or medical affairs.

It is easy to discount these external accoutrements as frivolous and superficial. I assure you that would be a mistake. People are judging you based on externals just as you are judging them.

Developing Executive Presence

I believe Executive Presence can be developed. When we break Executive Presence down into its basic components, we find there are many behaviors that can be strengthened. Much of the "aura" of Executive Presence is body language that communicates self-assuredness and confidence. A well-dressed man who walks into a room with his head held high, standing tall, wearing a friendly smile and offering a firm handshake commands attention and respect. On the other hand, a man who walks into a room shabbily dressed with his head bowed down, his hands in his pockets, looking at the floor will be quickly ignored and forgotten.

You can develop your Executive Presence by strengthening your visual and your vocal style.

Develop your visual style

The following components of visual style are important to strengthening your image:

Posture. Your shoulders should be square and your head held up, not down or tilted. Relax your shoulders, but keep your body erect. Rounded shoulders give a soft, weak, insecure impression.

Facial expressions. You don't need a fake smile on your face, but it should reflect a pleasant disposition. Some of you may remember how former president Jimmy Carter was criticized for having a permanent smile. This smile did not go over well when he was delivering bad news or serious information. You can't trust what an individual is saying when his facial expressions are not appropriate. It's important to know what your facial expressions are communicating when you are feeling a certain way. When I am listening intently or feeling critical, my facial expression gives it away because of my furrowed eyebrows. A senior executive would probably have no reaction to my intense listening, but if I'm speaking with a client or more junior person, it could be off-putting or intimidating.

Hence, when I'm feeling intense, I have trained myself to touch the muscles between my eyebrows and relax them.

Eye contact. This is your greatest opportunity to communicate comfort, acceptance, and affirmation. Whether you're speaking to a group, your boss, or a colleague, maintaining eye contact is important. Think about when you've spoken with someone who often looked away and could not maintain eye contact. How did it make you feel? There is no reason to lock on and stare, but there must be an easy give and take. Lack of eye contact is not an issue for people with Executive Presence.

Gestures. I think most people understand how important gestures are when giving a stand-up presentation, but they are sometimes even more important when you are sitting around a conference table or standing around in a networking session.

When people are nervous or uncomfortable, they tend to hold their hands and arms close to their body. They cross their arms, clasp their hands tightly, or shove their hands into their pockets. These are all sure signs of discomfort and will take away from your Executive Presence.

It's important to find a relaxed "home" or "default" position. This is the position you place your hands and arms in when you are not gesturing. Your hands can be down by your side or clasped gently in front of your body. You'll need to get in front of the mirror and practice to see what looks best on you. Check out the weathermen and women when they're standing and making idle chit-chat with their fellow reporters. They generally adopt a relaxed "home" position.

Stance. Your feet should be positioned no wider than your shoulders. If your stance is too wide, you look combative. Men tend to do this more than women. If it's too narrow, you look like you're trying to take up as little space as possible, which makes you appear timid and weak. This can be a challenge for many women.

Movement. Your movements should be smooth, graceful, and purposeful. We need to become aware of any unconscious twitching or nervous habits that others can see and we are not aware of. Remember John's jiggling of his leg? I've seen others heat up and become so intense that they start to pace around the room.

If you have access to a camcorder, tape yourself. If not, ask a good friend or trusted colleague to provide feedback after seeing you in action. This is the very best way to assess your visual technique.

Strengthening your vocal technique

I've worked with numerous leaders whose gifts and talents were not totally appreciated because of their voices. New York accents, foreign accents, speech impediments, southern drawls can all get in the way of an otherwise promising career. It is not a coincidence that some of our most famous and memorable orators have beautiful voices — Martin Luther King Jr. had a deep and resonant voice. Other compelling speakers come to mind, such as Barbara Jordan, Diane Sawyer, Liddy Dole, and James Earl Jones. Voice quality gives one a leg up when it comes to the vocal aspect of Executive Presence. But no matter what type of voice you have, you can refine your technique.

If people like what they see, they will then listen to your voice. If they like what they hear, they will then focus on what you have to say. Vocal technique consists of five components that you can develop to strengthen your Executive Presence. An audio recorder will help you evaluate the following components of vocal technique:

Rate of speech. We generally speak anywhere from 140–400 words per minute. Speech that is too slow can create an impression that you are a bit dull. And speech that is too fast can make one appear "slick" or slippery. Whether you are too slow or too fast can depend on what part of the country you live in. Fast talkers up North are hardly noticed, but their speech could be off-putting to people in the South. Slower speaking southerners can seem charming to some or just downright dull to others. You need to adapt accordingly. Pick up the pace a bit if you tend to be slow. If you speak quickly, your best bet is to pause more often as opposed to slowing down. We can understand when speech is spoken quickly but pausing gives the listener time to reflect and a sense that they are in a two-way conversation.

Articulation. High-level executives are usually quite articulate. Their words are crisp and easily understood. Articulation refers to the preciseness of sound. Martha Stewart is known for pronouncing each and every syllable. Picture her saying, "How prêt-tee and deli-cious these cook-kees are going to be." If your speech is sloppy, you can make a poor impression on others. People won't necessarily know that your s-t's or d-t's were not sharp, but they will come away with an impression or feeling that is less than positive. This is an area that is best evaluated by a professional speech coach. Before I started my business over 20 years ago, I contracted a few sessions with a speech coach. She was able to pick up a few subtleties and I worked on them. Those few sessions made an impact on my speaking skills, vocal technique, and confidence.

Pitch. This refers to the highness or lowness of sound. Women who speak in high-pitched voices are speaking from the vocal cord area in the throat as opposed to speaking from the diaphragm, where the sound is much richer and more resonant. A high-pitched voice sounds weak, meek, and timid.

Volume. This refers to the amplification of sound, i.e., loudness or softness. You will need to modulate this depending on the situation.

Use of nonwords. "Ah, uh, you know, okay" — these nonwords are usually used as filler. Some folks are uncomfortable with silence and they use these words to fill up the air time. Better to simply pause.

Foreign accents. People with foreign accents often believe they are at a disadvantage. This is not true as long as they are articulate and can be easily understood. If they are, I think they have an advantage because the difference causes people to pay more attention.

POWERFUL vs. powerless language. Powerful language is brief, direct, and to the point. The Gettysburg Address is an example of a powerful communication that is short, focused, and impactful. Speakers who are economic in their speech are far more desirable to listen to than are those who meander, get off track, and speak with powerless language.

Powerless language consists of hedging and using qualifiers such as: "maybe, perhaps, I'm not sure you'll agree with me." These statements diminish what you are saying as well as others' perception of you. If you are not confident in what you are saying, the listener will not be confident either.

Get help if you need it

Hire a professional image consultant. This is not fluff, ladies and gentlemen. A good image consultant will have an artistic flair but will also understand the technology involved in fine tuning one's image. A well-trained image consultant will help ensure that your hair, makeup, glasses, style of shirts, ties, slacks, dresses, etc., all reflect an image that is appropriate to the level you aspire to. I think this is particularly important in today's confusing climate of "business casual."

As I travel from organization to organization, I see a wide range of variations on the theme of business casual. I see blue jeans, khaki jeans, open-toed shoes, sleeveless shirts, and tight fitting tops and pants all posing as business casual. Better to err on the side of dressing too formally. A professional image consultant will be able to help you in that area.

Work with a speech coach. If you are concerned with presenting your best possible image in the workplace, schedule a consultation with a speech coach. Speech coaches help you improve your communication style so that people gain a more positive impression of you.

Get in shape. You can do this on your own or by working with a personal trainer. Working with a personal trainer will force you to get into the gym and work beyond your comfort zone. But you can certainly achieve an increased level of fitness working on your own. As you develop more strength aerobically and achieve muscular and skeletal development, more oxygen is pumped into the circulatory system, your muscles, and your brain. Hence, you increase your mental sharpness as well. We all know that exercise is good for your health. It gives you the stamina you need to work hard and the results produce confidence.

Learn from others. Observe the people around you who have Executive Presence. Note the type of clothing they wear, their posture, and their speech. Check out the way they interact with people. Create a list of your key observations. Review the list and rate yourself on a scale of 1 to 5 for each item. Give yourself a 5 for items that you have well under control and a 1 for items that need development. Use the list to identify two or three areas that you can focus on to strengthen your Executive Presence.

Complete the Total Image Strategy Checklist. I've talked a lot about working with an image consultant. If you are not able to do that, I've included a way for you to work on your own. For the past several years, I've worked with image consultant Carolyn Gustafson. She has helped many of my clients develop a strong Executive Presence and increased confidence. Carolyn has graciously agreed to allow me to include her *Total Image Strategy Checklist* in this book — see **Success Step 5.1** on page 114. You can complete this alone or with a trusted friend or colleague and evaluate how well you're doing in the areas of appearance, body language, voice, communication skills, business, and dining etiquette.

Success story

Ralph is an executive at a major financial institution in New York City. He was born and raised in a local housing project. Though smart, committed and talented, he recognized this was not enough to take him to the top. He hired a speech coach so he could lose his New York accent; he lost weight, got in shape, and upgraded his dress. His strategy worked. He made it to the top. Today, he is a man of tremendous influence.

Executive Presence is a lot of work, but it is attainable and your future depends on it.

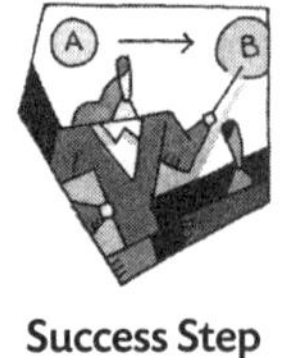

Success Step

Success Step 5.1 | Total Image Strategy Checklist

Appearance	**Good**	**Needs Work**
QUALITY CLOTHING		
Dark suit	☐	☐
Perfect fit	☐	☐
Perfect condition	☐	☐
Flattering style	☐	☐
Flattering color	☐	☐
Conservative classic style	☐	☐
Men: White ***long sleeve***	☐	☐
All cotton shirt	☐	☐
Silk tie: tied with dimple	☐	☐
Conservative pattern	☐	☐
QUALITY ACCESSORIES		
Bag	☐	☐
Belt	☐	☐
Jewelry	☐	☐
Simple watch	☐	☐
Men: Lace-up black shoes	☐	☐
Over-the-calf socks	☐	☐
Women: Closed-toe pump	☐	☐
Always wear hosiery	☐	☐
Up-to-date eyeglasses (reflection free)	☐	☐
IMPECCABLE GROOMING		
Odor free	☐	☐
Fragrance free	☐	☐
Hand/nails well manicured	☐	☐
Hair: Clean	☐	☐
Well cut	☐	☐
Women: Sophisticated style	☐	☐
Women: Moderate make-up	☐	☐
Men: Clean shaven	☐	☐
BODY LANGUAGE		
Smile	☐	☐
Stillness	☐	☐
Firm handshake	☐	☐
Sitting posture	☐	☐
Walking posture	☐	☐
Standing posture	☐	☐
Good eye contact	☐	☐
No nervous gestures	☐	☐
VOICE		
Free of slang	☐	☐
Pleasant tone	☐	☐
Vocal variety	☐	☐
Correct volume	☐	☐

Crisp articulation	☐	☐
Free of vocal static	☐	☐
Medium to low pitch	☐	☐
Volume	☐	☐
COMMUNICATION SKILLS		
Avoid swearing	☐	☐
Avoid interrupting	☐	☐
Avoid off-color jokes	☐	☐
Avoid inappropriate topics	☐	☐
React, relate, remember	☐	☐
Listen more than speak	☐	☐
Turn the conversation to others	☐	☐
Use tact and diplomacy	☐	☐
Ask open-ended questions	☐	☐
Put positive spin on comments	☐	☐
BUSINESS ETIQUETTE		
Punctual	☐	☐
Stand to shake hands	☐	☐
Always stand for introductions	☐	☐
Know how to make introductions	☐	☐
Respond to introductions	☐	☐
Introduce self	☐	☐
Telephone etiquette	☐	☐
Effective voice mail	☐	☐
Effective messages	☐	☐
Making a call	☐	☐
Write thank-you notes	☐	☐
Wear name tag on right side	☐	☐
DINING ETIQUETTE		
Hands above table	☐	☐
Know thy territory	☐	☐
Know napkin etiquette	☐	☐
Hold utensils correctly	☐	☐
Can respond to a toast	☐	☐
Silent when food is in mouth	☐	☐
Know sneeze and cough etiquette	☐	☐
Cut food in one direction only	☐	☐
Know the "rest" and "done" signals	☐	☐
Sit straight with elbows off table	☐	☐
Complain only away from others	☐	☐
Wait till others are served to begin	☐	☐
Cut one piece of meat at a time	☐	☐
Break and butter bread one bite at a time	☐	☐

You never get a second chance to make a first impression! First impressions last!

Carolyn Gustafson, AICI, CIP www.imagestrategy.com

CHAPTER 6
Managing Change

The events of 9/11, Anthrax, and the war in Iraq have changed the way we live our lives and view our world. Americans have transitioned from what we now know was a false sense of security to a heightened awareness of the constant threat of terrorism. While this change happened virtually overnight, adjusting to the emotional, psychological, and personal losses of these events may take years.

We also have to adjust to change in our personal lives. And sometimes various changes occur simultaneously. Before one transition is completed, another one begins. Just when your youngest child is off to college and you're looking forward to enjoying your empty nest, the oldest one announces that he is moving back home. There are unexpected health issues, the loss of a loved one, new arrivals, marriages, promotions, and relocations.

Change is occurring just as rapidly in the marketplace as well.

Between 1993 and 2003, nearly 50 percent of all U.S. companies were restructured. Over 80,000 firms were acquired or experienced a merger. At least 700,000 organizations sought bankruptcy protection. More than 450,000 organizations failed and more than 24 million jobs were lost. These corporate changes have affected the lives of millions of people.

In the next decade, at least one-quarter of all current knowledge and accepted business practices will be obsolete. The life span of new technology will decrease from the current 18 months. Women will own over 50 percent of all businesses in the United States. And entire industries will be replaced by ones that haven't yet been developed.

Further, 20 times as many people will be working at home; a majority of the entrants into the workforce will be women and minorities; dual career couples will increase to 63 percent of all families; and the growth and development of a One World Economy will further increase global competition. It's mind-boggling!

So what do we make of all this? Some 2,500 years ago the Greek philosopher, Heraclitus, said, "Change is the only constant." That statement is just as true today. I'd like to add that "change is constant and no one escapes." But we don't have to be victimized by change. The process of change is both predictable and manageable. And by understanding its effects, you can work through personal and career transitions from a position of strength and confidence as opposed to weakness and helplessness.

I am very confident that you have experienced some type of change in your life in the last 12 months. Let's examine how these changes affected you. Grab a pen to take a personal survey of the effects of these recent changes. **(Success Step 6.1)**

Success Step 6.1 | Personal Change Survey

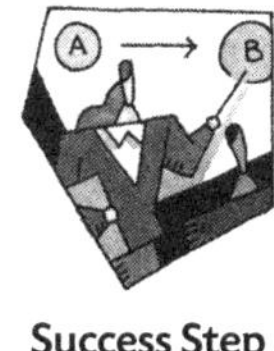

Success Step

Jot down changes you have experienced in the past 12 months in the following areas:

Work: ______________________________

____

____

Health: ______________________________

____

____

Family: ______________________________

____

____

Personal: ______________________________

____

____

Identify the one change that has caused you the greatest amount of stress. ________

____

____

Identify the one change that has caused you the least amount of stress. ________

____

- ☛ Jot down changes you have experienced in one of the following areas: Work, Health, Family, or Personal.
- ☛ Identify the one change that has caused you the greatest amount of stress.
- ☛ Identify the one change that caused you the least amount of stress.
- ☛ Compare the two. You will probably recognize that the change that caused you the least amount of stress is the one over which you had the greatest sense of control.

This is an important insight because to the extent that we normalize the process of change and understand that it is a predictable process, we gain a greater sense of control and experience less stress.

There is a time for everything and a season for every activity

In many parts of the country, the seasons change in a very dramatic way. In the Northeast, we experience some winters that are very intense and others that are relatively mild and uneventful. Similarly, our summers can either be unbearably hot and humid or relatively cool and enjoyable. We expect this year after year and prepare for the change. In the fall, we may put anti-freeze in our cars and caulking in our windows. In the spring, we make certain that our air conditioners are maintained and the filters are cleaned. We change our wardrobes to adapt to the temperature of the season. We control what we can, and then deal with the season as it unfolds.

The process of change

The process of change is deceivingly simple: first, there is an Ending, Middle and a New Beginning. Each stage is critical and must be fulfilled in order to move into the next. Change is the event. It is situational, outcome-focused, and relatively quick. Change happens when you transfer your child from one school to another, move into a new neighborhood, change jobs, end a relationship, hire or fire an employee, paint the living room, or buy a new car.

Transition, on the other hand, is the psychological experience of change. It is process-based, gradual, and slow. Moving to a new neighborhood means that we must cope with the loss of familiar activities, friends, patterns, and resources, and make the adjustment to new behaviors, new people, new places, and new activities. That takes time. It is often uncomfortable or downright painful. That is why transition is so difficult.

Futurist Marilyn Ferguson states:

> *"It's not so much that we're afraid of change or so in love with the old ways, but it's the place in between that we fear. It's like being in between trapezes. It's Linus when his blanket is in the dryer. There is nothing to hold on to."*

That place in between is scary and unsettling because things are not as they once were nor are they what they are going to be. Fear of the unknown is normal. Acknowledging your feelings and understanding that most people experience these fears helps alleviate some of the anxiety that change brings.

Dr. William Bridges is a premier and noted researcher in the area of change and transition. He defines the process of transition as having three phases: the Ending, the Neutral Zone, and the New Beginning. The Ending is the close or the death of the old way. The Neutral Zone is the soft, unstable place between the Ending and the New Beginning.

A time to die

Working through the Ending is probably the most challenging component of the entire phase of transition, because it is here that you have to let go of what is comfortable and familiar. Disengagement from your past is difficult. Many people suffer through disillusionment, disorientation, and a sense of disequilibrium. Things don't make sense. Not only is there no light at the end of the tunnel, there doesn't even seem to *be* a tunnel.

In working through the Ending you must understand very specifically what is lost and what isn't. Identify those losses that can be recovered, replaced, remodeled or redefined, as well as those that need to be relinquished. You may need to sit down and work this out with a friend.

I like the way my friend Lesa describes the Neutral Zone. She calls it the "Gray Area." I like this description because it describes the process within the process, i.e., moving from darker gray areas within the Neutral Zone to lighter ones where we ultimately can see our way out.

> *Recently, Lesa's organization went through a long and painful merger. Lesa was able to maintain and strengthen her position although the transition was emotionally draining. As a leader, she worked hard to help her team through both individual and organizational dynamics while simultaneously dealing with the same things herself.*

Because she understood the change process and the stages of transition that she and her team were experiencing, she was able to help them communicate their true feelings. She kept things in perspective for herself and her team, even when the ground below them was very soft. Their future responsibilities had not been assigned, new players were coming on the scene, and many things were up in the air.

Lesa made no attempt to dismiss their feeling of uneasiness, nor did she try to convince them there was no reason to be uncomfortable. She toed the corporate line and supported senior management, but was also available and encouraging to her staff. They understood that the captain was in control of the ship and learned that big ships turn around very slowly. She helped them understand that the Gray Area would be unsettling for a while and that everything they were feeling was normal. Her department made it through the transition period by taking one step one day at a time.

You may not have a Lesa to make that journey with you through the Neutral Zone. So let me share with you some of the pitfalls and opportunities to look for.

A time to mourn

Take the time to mourn your loss. I've known people who, after losing their jobs, attempted to leap from the Ending to the New Beginning in a single bound. They were in such a hurry to move on and to avoid the Neutral Zone that they made bad decisions about the next move in their careers.

I realize that sometimes, because of the financial needs of your family or because of mounting bills, you just do what you must do. Nevertheless, it is important to understand and allow yourself a time of mourning. Take a few days off, talk to a good friend about what you're feeling and thinking. There is no reason to pretend to be strong when, in truth, you are hurting.

Taking a symbolic piece of the past with you into the future can help bring closure to the past, but sometimes it is important to bury it. Funerals and memorial services are ways that we, the living, can bring closure to a cherished relationship. Similarly, a ceremony of some sort is often helpful to bring finality to the ending areas of our lives. In the workplace, goodbye parties and recognition ceremonies serve to bring closure to the past.

I belong to a professional association that recently underwent a change of leadership. The final years of the old regime were frustrating and discouraging. I removed 10 years of awards and plaques from my work area because they represented pain to me in the Ending stage of my transition. I simply put them in a box and stored them in my garage. Today, the association's leadership is first class. Now I proudly display in my office the latest plaques I have received as well as photos taken with the organization's president.

A time to heal...a time to mend

The Neutral Zone is often a period of frightening emptiness. The death of a loved one, the loss of a job, a divorce, or relocation can cause you to experience a huge void in your life. The Neutral Zone is about totally letting go of the past and the old self (Disintegration) and building a new self (Reintegration). This is the source of renewal that leads you into the New Beginning.

We often see the people in the process of reinventing themselves in the entertainment industry, where performers sometimes make radical changes in order to attract new audiences and maintain popularity. But for most people, reinventing themselves is not a strategic move, but a result of circumstances beyond their control — such as a job layoff, illness, or the end of a marriage.

Harry Davis is a brilliant artist whose works have been purchased by many celebrities. He is the first to admit that he may have never become the artist he is today had he not become a paraplegic at age 19. Harry was injured in the army and went from being a muscular paratrooper with the 82nd Airborne, to a meager 149-pound defeated, depressed young man.

He wallowed in the Neutral Zone for many years, refusing to accept that he would never walk again. Hence, Harry couldn't move forward. Each night he'd dream the same type of dream — where he was lost, either in some strange town, in a hospital, or in a school. The dreams were always dark and gloomy and he was unable to remember where he was going or how to find his way. He was very depressed.

During this time, Harry's mother bought him a paint-by-numbers kit. He enjoyed painting. It was something to do and took his mind off of his problems. He began to paint more and more.

In time, Harry successfully worked through the grieving process to the Acceptance Stage. He started to work with his doctors and adopted a healthy diet. He began to work out. He studied karate and got involved in wheelchair racing. Soon the dreams stopped. Eventually, Harry even went back to college, graduating with a degree in sociology and preparing for a career in social work. Then something miraculous happened — Harry sold a painting. He buckled down and started to take his craft seriously. He essentially reinvented himself and it all came about in the Neutral Zone.

Now Harry is grateful for the accident. He admits that without having experienced that tragic event he would not be the man he is today. He would be different, but not necessarily better. He has a beautiful wife, a loving family, and great friends. By all accounts, Harry is a happy and successful man. He is grateful that either by accident or by God's plan, he has found his true purpose in life. He likes who he is and what he does. He touches many lives, both through his work and by his example.

A time to refrain

It is in the Neutral Zone that you begin to view life from the standpoint of what's really important and what isn't.

When Joe Torre, manager of the New York Yankees, was diagnosed with cancer, he had to be away from the World Championship team for a few months. When he returned, a reporter asked him whether he thought about baseball during his recuperation. Torre responded that not only had he not thought about baseball during that time, he said that he didn't even care about it. The most meaningful things to him during that time were his health and his family.

The Neutral Zone experience is a good opportunity to take some time alone to reevaluate what you really want in life. This can be tough if you've recently been downsized and you are concerned about the financial strain the loss of work is going to cause you. Do what you need to do, but recognize the importance of this phase in facilitating the onset of the next. I wish I could give you 3–5 simple steps that would help you negotiate your way though the Neutral Zone at warp-speed. Regretfully, I cannot. But the following steps will help you feel more secure and confident as you walk through it:

Get away for a few days. This is ideal but not always feasible. So figure out another way to take time for you. Go to a local park or to the waterfront, wherever you can be alone with few distractions. It is in that quiet space that you can hear the still, small voice within. It is here where you can listen and look for clues and messages that direct you to where you should be moving next. Step back and take stock. Begin to create and hold an image of your desired outcome and take the time to write down your ideas.

Create areas of control in your life. Identify what you have control over. Perhaps you have lost your job. While that is out of your control, there are many things that are still within your control. For example, be sure to continue your daily routines of exercise and grooming. Become more involved in the lives of your children and their activities. In other words, compartmentalize the item you have no control over so that it doesn't negatively affect other areas of your life.

Stay current. Read newspapers, periodicals, and use the Internet to stay current about trends in your field of interest. Maintaining a fresh understanding of the world around you will help your decision making about taking your next step.

Stay connected to your support network. If possible, continue membership in professional organizations, join a support group, or gain support from people in your community, your church, and your family.

Clarify your sense of purpose. Discuss your ideas about taking next steps with friends, family, and colleagues. Your direction can become clearer to you when you seek advice from caring people.

Keep a journal of your activities and feelings. Writing down your activities and feelings is a great way to track your progress. It allows you to see how you are moving through the shades of gray.

How do we manage and find meaning in the Neutral Zone? Go with the flow. Surrender to the process and let the process work you.

A time to laugh...and a time to dance

How do we operate in the New Beginning? Stop readying yourself and act! There are very specific actions you can take.

- Convert your visions and dreams into action plans by writing them down.
- Study the plan, create a path that will facilitate the plan, and then evaluate whether you have the skill to achieve the plan. If not...
    - ☛ Take a course or hire a consultant to work with you.
    - ☛ Break the plan into small steps with realistic time frames.
    - ☛ Focus your efforts on getting a few quick successes.
    - ☛ Take a step-by-step, incremental approach to begin to identify yourself with the final result, or the New Beginning.
    - ☛ See yourself there; visualize it.

As you're moving toward the New Beginning, keep a positive attitude. Also, try to increase your flexibility and tolerance for risk and stress. You can assess your tolerance by completing **Success Strategy 6.2 Managing Change, Managing Self Checklist**. Review the opposing descriptions. Circle the number that is most like you.

Success Strategy 6.2 | Managing Change, Managing Self Checklist

MOST LIKE ME																MOST LIKE ME
Yielding and Flexible	7	6	5	4	3	2	1	0	1	2	3	4	5	6	7	Unyielding and Inflexible
Creative and Original	7	6	5	4	3	2	1	0	1	2	3	4	5	6	7	Traditional
Risk Taker	7	6	5	4	3	2	1	0	1	2	3	4	5	6	7	Risk Averse
Handle Stress	7	6	5	4	3	2	1	0	1	2	3	4	5	6	7	Does Not Handle Stress

Managing Change, Managing Self Tips

Increase Your Flexibility

1. Avoid perfectionist language, e.g., should, must, never
2. Ask more questions
3. Listen and consider the thoughts and ideas of others

Increase Your Creativity

1. Schedule time to think
2. Brainstorm ideas with others
3. Ask "what if" questions
4. Step out of your comfort zone

Increase Your Risk Taking

1. Stop being so conciliatory
2. Practice pushing back
3. Set small incremental goals

Increase Your Ability to Manage Stress

1. Exercise
2. Take time for yourself
3. Schedule quiet time each day
4. Access your personal support system (friends, family, trusted colleagues, faith)

Individual change

Just as there are predictable and manageable transitions that we go through in our personal growth and development, e.g., the "terrible 2s," puberty, adolescence, and menopause, the dynamics of individual and organizational change follow a predictable path through four phases: Denial, Resistance, Exploration, and Adaptation.

> ***Denial.*** The first response to change is often shock or disbelief. The mind protects itself from being overwhelmed by refusing to recognize the information. Sooner or later the impact will hit home and a personal response is required.
>
> ***Resistance.*** Things seem to get worse during this phase. It is common to be angry and spend time blaming and complaining. Personal distress levels rise, possibly resulting in physical, emotional, or mental symptoms.
>
> ***Exploration.*** After a period of struggle, there is openness to new information; you begin clarifying goals, assessing priorities, and exploring alternatives. A shift has occurred to a more positive, hopeful mindset.
>
> ***Adaptation.*** When you have successfully committed yourself to a new course of action, adaptation has occurred.

These stages do not necessarily have firm beginnings and endings. They can overlap, and not everyone will experience them in the same way. You can't force your way through them. This is an emotional and psychological process and these stages will have to play themselves out. This is why journaling and talking with trusted friends can help. You don't want to go through this alone, and friends can help you assess what stage you are in and how you are moving through the process.

Organizational change

Organizational change has the same set of predictable dynamics. But the effects are magnified because the stakes are high and so many people and processes are involved. You can expect virtually everything in your workplace to take a dip during times of organizational transition. Typically, communication deteriorates and productivity suffers. People are less concerned with their colleagues or the organization. Their focus becomes, "What will happen to me?" Hence, there is often a loss of team-play, because people become inwardly focused and self-centered. Power struggles and turf issues often arise. And a number of good people will likely bail out.

In his book, *Iococca*, Lee Iococca, former CEO of Chrysler Corporation, discusses how, despite his enormous success at turning around the failing behemoth, he was regretful that so many good people were lost. Yet, this is an unavoidable aspect of change.

If you're a leader, this is not the time to bury your head in the sand. Your people need to know as much about what's going on as you do, even if that is very little. They need to feel that you're concerned with their welfare as well as the good of the organization. If you're not a leader, you must manage your participation in water cooler discussions and rumors. Again, recognize that the feelings of loss, uncertainty, distrust, isolation, and devaluation are normal and temporary. Tie a knot in the rope and hang on...this too will pass.

The Chinese character for crises consists of two parts: one signifies danger and the other opportunity. This is the dichotomy of change. It can be frightening to spread your wings over the vast abyss of the unknown. Still, opportunities to advance your career and to increase your personal development come in no better package than the form of that old and constant friend: change.

Action plan

Convert the relevant and appropriate actions into concrete steps that you can take in the next few days and weeks. **(Success Step 6.3)**

Success Step 6.3 | Personal Actions for Change

Action Plan

Work: ____________________

____

____

____

Health: ____________________

____

____

____

Family: ____________________

____

____

____

Personal: ____________________

____

____

____

CHAPTER 7
Who's Who in the Workplace Lineup

Understanding and learning how to relate to people is critically important for the individual who wishes to bolster his or her influence in the workplace. Some folks are naturally gregarious and seem to have an easier time engaging diverse groups of people. Others struggle in this area, hiding within the safety of their office or cubicle so that no one notices them or expects them to communicate. You don't have to be born with a special gift to be an effective people person. It's simply a matter of understanding the impact of certain behavior styles.

Successful people are people who understand themselves and how their behavior affects others. They tend to have a positive attitude and they know how to be flexible, adapting their behavior to different situations and to different people. In this chapter, you will discover your specific behavioral style as well as the styles of others. You will also learn how various behavior styles operate. You should finish this chapter with an awareness of how to read the behavior of others as well as how to become more flexible with your own style.

Not long ago, I conducted a workshop in a hotel on the beautiful island of Bermuda with my colleague, Pam. We were using her laptop computer. At the end of day one, we stored the battery pack in the hotel's conference room cabinet. When we returned the next morning, we couldn't find it. Pam became worried and annoyed and suggested that someone had probably taken it.

"Oh, no," I said. "No one would have taken it. That's just silly. Who would steal it? And besides, if it is missing, we can always talk to Glenn, the maitre'd. I'm sure he'll find it for us."

"No," she replied. "He's not going to want to help us."

Pam was quite cynical about the possibility of finding the battery pack, although I assured her that if Glenn couldn't help us, the manager of the hotel would. I further assured her that even if the manager could not help, the coordinators of the program would certainly reimburse her for the loss. Nevertheless, Pam was convinced and adamant that her property had been stolen.

I thought to myself, "Pam is certainly being unnecessarily negative. After all, everyone here is so nice." Well, she was right.

Her battery pack was never returned and she was never compensated for it.

What fascinates me about this scenario is how differently we perceived the situation and how our perceptions were reflective of our respective behavioral styles. My style is one that tends to be eternally optimistic. I oftentimes miss the negative aspects of situations that could be important factors in a decision-making process. Pam's style is one of cautious concern about being taken advantage of. She tends to be suspicious in situations where that behavior may not be warranted. Her style comes across as a little heavy-handed when dealing with others who may have no intention of harming or cheating her. Is one style right or better? No, just different.

In the 1940s Dr. William Marston wrote a book called *The Emotions of Normal People.* His book identified a four-factor behavioral style model. These behavioral styles were labeled as Dominance, Influence, Supportiveness, and Conscientiousness. From that work, Dr. John Geyer developed an assessment instrument in the early 1970s called the Personal Profile System, which is based on the same four-factor model, DISC.

Marston's original work described human behavior as a result of two intersecting factors, namely, how we see ourselves in an environment and how we feel about ourselves. People will either see themselves as powerful or less than powerful in an environment, and perceive the environment as either favorable or less than favorable. **(Illustration 7.1)**

Illustration 7.1

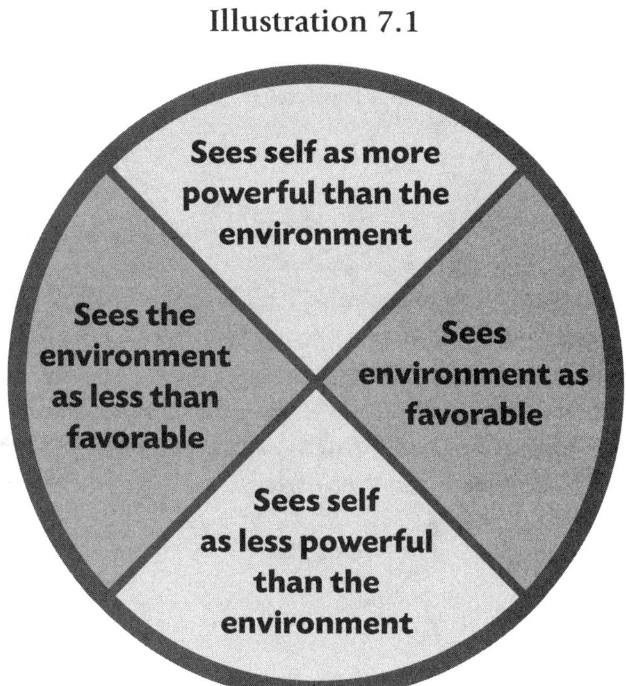

Illustration

During my Bermuda workshop with Pam, I perceived the environment as favorable — friendly, honest, and open. But once I learned that the environment in which we were working was not that way, I began locking up my things. Pam perceived the environment as unfavorable — dishonest, unfriendly, and suspicious. And she will likely continue viewing it that way because of what happened.

Let's look at how behavioral styles develop. (**Illustration 7.2**)

Illustration

Illustration 7.2

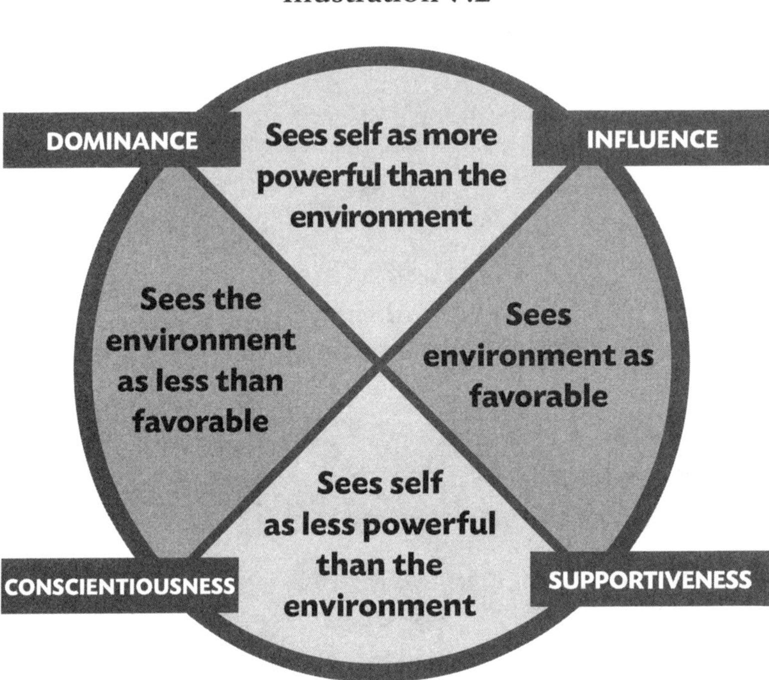

Dominance. A person who perceives herself as more powerful than the environment and who sees the environment as unfavorable will attempt to manage the environment in a direct, aggressive style. This style is identified as Dominance.

Influence. Someone who perceives himself as more powerful than the environment and who also sees the environment as favorable will attempt to manage their environment by influencing people. This behavioral style is called Influence.

Supportiveness. Those who see the environment as favorable but see themselves as less powerful than the environment will be a little more laid-back, a bit quieter than the D-Style and the I-Style described above. They manage their environment by cooperating with others. This style is called Supportiveness.

Conscientiousness. People who see the environment as unfavorable but see themselves as less powerful than the environment will develop a style that allows them to work within the existing structure to produce outcomes that are very accurate and precise. They control their environment through accurate performance. This is the Conscientiousness style.

What is your behavioral style?

For you to obtain an accurate and valid reading of your behavioral style, you will need to take the Personal Profile Assessment. You can do this online by logging onto my website at **www.readysetgrow.biz.**

Can we really pigeonhole people?

DISC is a great model for understanding behavior. Nevertheless, we're looking at a four-factor analysis that divides people into categories. The idea that we will pigeonhole people may make you a bit uncomfortable. I understand your concern. Assessment instruments can never assess the sum total of an individual's behavior patterns. They do not take into account what people have learned, their values, how they've grown, or the degree to which they're willing to be flexible. Different instruments will also measure different things, but they can be quite useful as they can provide a sense of how people like to relate to others and to their environment. Let's forge ahead using this instrument as a tool for greater insight and understanding.

Style description

If you've taken the Personal Profile Assessment, you now know your behavioral style. If you haven't, you may be able to guess your style based on the descriptions that follow.

We are each born with a unique personality. Once that core personality begins to experience the world around it, preferences for behavioral styles develop. The result of your Personal Profile Assessment reflects your behavior within a particular environment. Generally, the behavioral styles experience their environment in the following ways:

> The Dominance behavioral style will see an environment that they want to overcome. So they try to change, fix, or control things.

The Influence style will see an environment they can influence and they'll do that through persuasion, promoting, or influencing others.

The Supportiveness style will see an environment they want to maintain and so they try to be cooperative, supportive, and agreeable in order to keep things stable.

The Conscientiousness style will see an unfavorable environment they do not want to change, but they'll work within the existing structure and the established rules, guidelines and procedures to ensure accuracy and quality.

DISC in detail

Let's understand the behavioral styles in greater detail.

Dominance (D-Style). D-Styles make things happen. They are driven individuals. They cause action. These people love challenges and they don't mind managing trouble. They enjoy taking charge, making quick decisions, and getting immediate results. They enjoy prestige, power, authority, and opportunities that lead to individual accomplishment. They also want to be free of others' supervision and control.

The flip side is that in their zeal to achieve results, they are often insensitive to other people. They step on toes and leave bodies in their wake. Also, they are not particularly detail-oriented. Don't launch into lengthy explanations when working with Dominants, you'll lose them.

Your Dominant Work Profile — Your strength as co-worker or team member is that you make decisions when others cannot. You confront the tough issues or situations. You accept change as a personal challenge; and, you keep your team focused and on task. Others may see limitations because you:

- ☛ May come across as unapproachable
- ☛ Can be insensitive to others
- ☛ Show impatience with others
- ☛ Try to move the team before it is ready

To be more effective you might try to:

- ☛ Develop more patience when working with others. Impatience is probably one of the most challenging issues for the D-Style to overcome.
- ☛ Tone down your directness and ask more questions. Remember reading in Chapter 4 about Adult behavior and asking questions? Your

Dominant Style may tend to have a tone that would be perceived as Critical Parent behavior. We know from our previous reading that people are usually put off by that.

☛ Work on your body language so that you appear more approachable. And offer encouragement as part of your interaction with others.

Influence (I-Style). I-Styles enjoy people. They enjoy meeting people, entertaining people, and participating in groups. They shape their environment by influencing and persuading others. They make good coaches and counselors as they are good at creating a motivational environment. These popular types enjoy social recognition and freedom from detail and control.

On the flip side (because of their enjoyment of people, fun, and stories), they may tend to focus more on people and less on tasks and details. They can sometimes be disorganized and are often late.

Your Influence Work Profile — If you have an Influence behavioral style, your strength as a co-worker or a team member may be that you are available to others. You inspire others. You spread your enthusiasm to others and give positive feedback to your colleagues.

Others may see limitations because you may be:

☛ Disorganized
☛ Superficial in your approach
☛ Lacking follow-through

You can be more effective by:

☛ Listening more carefully
☛ Becoming more organized
☛ Providing more detail

Supportiveness (S-Style). The S-Style wants to cooperate with others and maintain the status quo in carrying out tasks. They are extraordinarily good at listening, demonstrating patience, loyalty, helping others, and creating a stable workplace environment. They enjoy predictable routines and stable environments. While they don't toot their own horns, they do appreciate credit for the work they've done. They tend to be homebodies, enjoying the stability of family life and close friends. As a result, they don't allow their work to infringe very much on their home life because it's too important to them.

The downside for people with the Supportiveness Style is that because of their strong need for stability and their interest in maintaining the status quo, they can be slow to change when change is warranted. Hence, they will stay too long in jobs and relationships when it's time to move on. Their key challenge is to balance their need for stability with the organizational need to grow, recognizing that growth means change, although change is uncomfortable for them.

Your Supportiveness Work Profile — If you exhibit S-Style behaviors, your strength as a co-worker or a team member may be that you are a good team player, someone who is likable. You are sensitive to the needs of others, you handle tasks methodically, and you are a good listener.

Others may see limitations because you may be:

- Indecisive
- Indirect
- Resistant to change

You can be more effective by:

- Becoming more assertive and direct
- Learning to accept change more readily by becoming willing to move out of your comfort zone
- Resisting the temptation to carry the burden of everyone else's problems, which they are more than happy to give you

Conscientiousness (C-Style). People with the C-Style are analytical thinkers. They work conscientiously within existing circumstances and structures to ensure quality. They concentrate on key details, ask lots of questions, and want to make sure that things are done correctly. They have extremely high standards based on quality and accuracy. That makes them critical of their own performance as well as others'. C-Styles can be very diplomatic, preferring a reserved, business-like atmosphere. If you tend to be a little chatty and you're meeting with someone who has this behavioral style, tone it down. His or her preference is to get right down to business.

On the flip side, the C-Style could learn to warm up in certain circumstances, relax, and go with the flow, because other styles have other preferences. They also need to learn that 100 percent accuracy is not always possible or desirable, given certain time constraints. The workplace is fluid, and the C-Style's passion for quality can delay results.

Your Conscientiousness Work Profile — If you are a C-Style, your strength as a co-worker or a team member may be that you:

- ☛ Are thorough
- ☛ Follow standards
- ☛ Emphasize accuracy
- ☛ Use diplomacy

Others may see limitations because you can be:

- ☛ Overly concerned with perfection
- ☛ Perceived as aloof, and as someone who hampers the creativity of others because you stick to the rules

You can be more effective by:

- ☛ Accepting different work styles
- ☛ Focusing on communication
- ☛ Working on relationships

Teams are most effective when they share in a diversity of styles and when team members realize, respect and honor those differences.

People reading

Our ability to relate to others and to get along with people depends on our ability to connect with them in a meaningful way. By understanding how others prefer to communicate, you gain insight on how to adjust your behavior when dealing with them. But how do we determine their behavioral style? Handing each person at your workplace an assessment would make you look like the office loon. Don't worry. There *is* a quick and simple way to assess someone's behavior style. Let's refer to **Illustration 7.3** on the following page.

Illustration

Illustration 7.3

	Active, Outgoing		
Task Oriented	D	I	People Oriented
	C	S	
	Quiet, Reserved		

The chart identifies the "D" and the "I" behavioral styles as Active and Outgoing, whereas the "C" and the "S" are Quiet and Reserved. You can begin to do people reading just by observing these basic characteristics. Ask yourself whether the individual you're assessing is active and outgoing or more quiet and reserved? Your answer will tell you if they are D/ I or S/C.

Our chart also identifies the "D" and the "C" as Task-oriented and the "I" and "S" as People-oriented. Ask yourself if the person is Task-oriented or People-oriented? Your response will tell you if they are D/C or I/S.

Let's profile someone we all know, the former mayor of New York City, Rudolph Giuliani. We begin by asking the question, is this man Active and Outgoing or Quiet and Reserved? There is no question about the answer. There is nothing quiet about Rudy. Clearly he is active and outgoing. The next question is this: is Rudy Giuliani Task-oriented or People-oriented? I think most New Yorkers would agree that he is Task-oriented. Refer to **Illustration 7.3**.

Because former Mayor Giuliani is Active and Outgoing we know he is either a "D" or an "I," and, because he is Task-oriented, he is either a "D" or a "C."

By plugging this information into our chart we can see that Mayor Giuliani's behavioral style is going to fall in the Dominance quadrant.

During the catastrophic events of September 11, 2001, it was Mayor Giuliani's focus on tasks and control that helped steer New York City back on course. While things seemed to be falling apart, he rose to the occasion and took charge. That gave many New Yorkers a great sense of comfort. In that circumstance, the Dominant behavioral style was appropriate and effective.

Refer back to **Illustration 7.3**. I'd like you to profile someone you view as a difficult person in your workplace or in your family. For whatever reason, you just don't click with this person as well as with other people. Once again, ask yourself the question, is this person Active and Outgoing or Quiet and Reserved? Also, is the person Task-oriented or People-oriented? Jot down your responses on the worksheet and determine their style.

Now that you understand their behavioral style and yours, on a separate piece of paper brainstorm some things that you can do to better relate to that individual.

With a little practice you will be able to profile others in your mind very quickly. Please remember that it's best to keep this information under your hat. If you think you've got someone pigeonholed, please don't share it with them — they may not appreciate it. Your goal in understanding the behavior of others is to know how to adjust *your* behavior to better relate to them.

Different equals different

One of the values in understanding behavioral styles is to recognize that people are different. We know this intellectually, but we often tend to look at people who think and behave differently than we do as wrong, bad, or more than stupid. However, it is important that we appreciate others' styles. Frankly, it's much easier to relate to and get along with people who are similar to us because we respond similarly in a given environment. I enjoy connecting with someone who really likes people because I like people. But does it mean that all other styles are bad? Of course not. But appreciating and working with other styles in a way that maximizes their impact is the key to greater effectiveness in your organization.

Appreciating other styles

Refer to **Success Step 7.1**. In the appropriate space, identify what you appreciate about the other three styles. So if you're an S-Style, jot down what it is that you appreciate about the "D," "I," and "C" Styles, and so on.

Success Step

Success Step 7.1 | Appreciating Other Styles

My Style is ________________

Appreciating Other Styles		
Style	Style	Style
________	________	________
________	________	________
________	________	________
________	________	________
________	________	________
________	________	________
________	________	________
________	________	________
________	________	________

Now let's look at how we can be more flexible with the other styles. See **Success Step 7.2,** What the Other Styles Need More of or Less of from Me. Think about what you need to do to give them what *they* need. For example, if I'm an S-Style, a D-Style person may need less of my adherence to status quo and more flexibility in terms of my willingness to accept change and move forward. The I-Style would need less detail from me and the C-Style may need less recognition from me.

Success Step 7.2 | What the Other Styles Need More of or Less of from Me

Success Step

My Style is ________________

What Do They Need "More of/Less of" from Me		
Style	Style	Style
________________	________________	________________
________________	________________	________________
________________	________________	________________
________________	________________	________________
________________	________________	________________
________________	________________	________________
________________	________________	________________
________________	________________	________________
________________	________________	________________

Flexing my style

A few pages ago, you identified a person with whom you have a challenging relationship. In **Success Step 7.3** (below) identify how you are going to adjust or "flex" your style to be effective with that particular person. Do more than one person if you'd like.

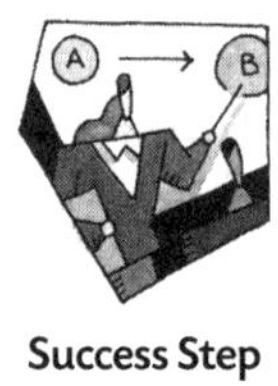

Success Step

Success Step 7.3 | Flexing My Style

Name of the individual with whom I have a challenge

____

How am I going to "flex" my style to be more effective with this person?

Working with behavioral styles takes some time. Getting used to it may be a slow process, but in time you will internalize the information and automatically begin profiling and responding appropriately to people with various styles. I wish you good effort with it. For a more detailed understanding of your behavioral style, please visit my website at **www.readysetgrow.biz**.

CHAPTER 8
Finding the Truth About Your Performance

If the Truth Shall Set You Free, Why Is It So Hard to Find?

Mac was the chief engineer of a major television network. He was a strong, decisive, and well-liked leader. When I coached him, I heard very positive feedback from all who worked for and with him. There was just one little issue that kept popping up. He had a habit of dropping the letter "s" off of verbs. He would say things like, "That sound bad." Apparently this is not uncommon in the region of the country where Mac grew up, but it did not play well in New York City. In the feedback interviews, I heard comments like "He speaks poor English," and "His communication skills aren't good." One person even perceived Mac as a poor writer.

During one of our conferences I pointed out to Mac that his speech often reflected a lack of agreement between subject and verb. "No one has ever told me that before," he responded. When he asked his wife about it, she reluctantly confessed, "Yes honey, you do that."

Mac was 54 years old and unfortunately his story is not uncommon. I have worked with countless clients who, when presented developmental feedback, responded as Mac did, saying, *"No one has ever told me that."* It's tragic that people are allowed to go through much or even their entire careers without the feedback they need to adjust and fine-tune their behavior to become more effective. Their true gifts and talents remain underdeveloped merely because they did not receive the appropriate feedback. It's tragic, unnecessary, and as a Leadership Development coach, drives me nuts. Thankfully, the situation is steadily improving. You can now find various types of feedback in the workplace. There is 360-degree Feedback, Upward Feedback, and even Peer Coaching. Nevertheless, it is still difficult for people to receive quality feedback.

My objective in this chapter is to help you understand:

- Why people can't share the whole truth
- What *is* the honest truth
- What are some ways to get the truth

Why is telling the truth so difficult?

How do you respond when your partner or your Mom asks, "Do I look fat in this outfit?" Or when your boss asks for your opinion on one of his ideas about which you feel lukewarm or even antagonistic? How many times have you read glowing performance reviews about employees whose performance is marginal at best?

Most of us find it easy to tell someone that it's time they considered taking an accounting class or a seminar to help them strengthen their presentation skills. But when it comes to the softer skills of style, communication, manner, and relationships, giving feedback is much more difficult. Here are some reasons why:

- You don't know how the person you're speaking to is going to react to the feedback.
- You're not confident that your delivery style will help the person to focus on changing the behavior, rather than on the likely wounds to his or her self-esteem.
- People are extraordinarily sensitive and can become defensive.
- The person you're attempting to help may have so many positive characteristics that bringing up the negative ones may appear petty.

Giving feedback takes time and hard work. And it must be done in a sensitive manner. Most people in the workplace are busy driving toward results. It is not unusual for feedback and other people-related issues to be perceived as distractions. So be warned: if you are not hearing anything negative about your performance, you can't be absolutely certain that you don't have a few flat sides. Even people in leadership positions may not be aware of their shortcomings.

Can you imagine an athlete spending his or her entire career practicing and competing without getting feedback from the coach? Of course not. Athletes recognize the importance of feedback — it helps refine their skills. Similarly, you need feedback if you're going to grow.

When I coach a client, I interview at least a dozen people, e.g., current and former bosses, colleagues, and followers. I ask everyone the same basic set of questions about my client's career potential, strengths and attributes, and areas of weakness.

Over the course of 20 years, I have conducted thousands of such interviews. I've taken a sampling of those interviews to identify the common themes. I present them here to help you identify areas on which you may focus. I have categorized five major areas of concern. These are: Self-Management, Relationship Management, Executive Presence, Leadership, and Listening.

Self-Management

People who have strong Self-Management skills are perceived as comfortable in their own skin. They possess a confident manner and a relaxed style. These people remain cool during conflicts and are not perceived as trying too hard or as always going full-throttle. It is not that they don't have drive or edginess, but they manage these attributes in a very unobtrusive way. Strong Self-Managers are very approachable. They manage their time well, are personally organized, and keep the envy demon at bay.

Relationship Management

Making a connection with people is important to those who are proficient in Relationship Management skills. These people appear to have a genuine interest in people and their activities beyond the workplace. They have a zest for life, a good sense of humor, and the type of charisma that draws people to them. Strong Relationship Managers are sensitive to people's needs and treat all people as persons, as opposed to nonpersons. They have excellent communication skills, including listening, speaking, facilitating, maintaining eye contact, and holding a steady tone of voice. They are also excellent team players.

Executive Presence

Executive Presence is part of your image. It includes the way you dress, your posture, and your overall appearance. People who possess Executive Presence are comfortable with themselves and with people at all levels in the organization. They have a genuine self-confidence and recognize that the workplace is a stage — people are watching and they need to put their best foot forward. I discuss Executive Presence extensively in Chapter 5.

Leadership

People with strong Leadership skills are not afraid to take a stand or initiative. They are strategic thinkers, creative, and visionary. Leaders recognize that their success comes from the success of their team. Hence, the development of their people is a high priority. Good leaders recognize that their work style may be different from others and do not impose their style by virtue of their position. They are patient with others, use their influence and collaboration skills to meet goals, and balance their focus on results with the global needs of the organization.

Listening

Good listeners have open minds. They are receptive to ideas that are different from their own. They do not make up their minds before hearing others out. Strong listeners don't interrupt others when they are speaking. Nor do they impatiently wait for their turn to speak. Rather, they are genuinely interested in what the other person has to say. They recognize that allowing others to finish their thoughts is not only good manners but also affirming. The speaker has their undivided attention.

Now that you understand the major areas of concern, how do you get feedback about your performance in these areas?

Perhaps the most obvious way to get feedback is to ask for it. I caution you to be judicious about whom you seek feedback from and how often. Feedback should come from someone you trust, and from someone who won't take your concerns to the water cooler. If you ask for feedback too often, you may be perceived as insecure or unsure of yourself.

I want to share with you an exercise that allows you to get feedback *without* having a direct conversation with someone. I have two versions of this exercise.

Version I: *General image*

This is a perception exercise that allows you to get feedback about your behavior without having a direct conversation with someone. Here's what I'd like you to do: refer to the illustration below.

Illustration

Illustration 8.1

Feedback Items

(Write in your preferences if you like)

Confident	Poised	Sophisticated	Approachable
Accessible	Charismatic	Personable	Sensitive
Self-aware	Diplomatic	Polished	Intense
Conceptual	Strategic	Visionary	Creative
Influential	Collaborative	Results-oriented	Open

The first step is to identify no less than seven and no more than fifteen items on which you want feedback. These items are taken from the five major areas of concern discussed above. You may wish to include your own feedback items, use the ones provided, or focus on only one or two areas. Take your time and highlight the items on which you want to focus. Once you've completed that, refer to **Success Step 8.1** and write in Column I the items you've just highlighted.

Success Step

Success Step 8.1

COLUMN I **Feedback Items** *(Write in your preferences if you like)*	COLUMN II **"I think they think I..."**	COLUMN III **"They should think I..."**
1. Confident	am extremely confident	
2. Approachable	am approachable	
3. Personable	am personable	
4. Sensitive	am more sensitive than I used to be	
5. Self-aware	am self-aware	
6. Conceptual	am very conceptual	
7. Influential	am very influential	
8. Collaborative	could work this a bit more	
9. Results-oriented	achieve results but at a cost	
10. Open	am sufficiently open	

Column II — I Think They Think.
Here you are going to identify what you think the "outside world" thinks of you regarding the feedback items in Column I. The "outside world" represents the people in your workplace. When you think about the "outside world" don't focus on a specific person. Rather, see a gray, amorphous "them" or "they." Write what you think "they" actually think of you regarding the first item on your list. Be truthful and specific.

Complete Column II by writing what you think the "outside world" thinks of you on all the items in Column I. Take your time with this exercise. You may need more than one sitting to complete it.

Column III — What They Should Think If They Knew the Real Me.
You have indicated what you think the "outside world" thinks of you in Column II. Now I'd like you to write what you think they should think if they knew the real you. Again, be as specific as possible. (Your worksheet should look something like **Success Step 8.2** below.)

Success Step 8.2

Success Step

COLUMN I **Feedback Items** *(Write in your preferences if you like)*	COLUMN II **"I think they think I..."**	COLUMN III **"They should think I..."**
Confident	am extremely confident	often doubt myself
Approachable	am approachable	am a very shy person
Personable	am personable	like people
Sensitive	am more sensitive than I used to be	am very sensitive
Self-aware	am self-aware	have to work at this
Conceptual	am very conceptual	am very conceptual
Influential	am very influential	am extremely influential
Collaborative	could work this a bit more	find this difficult because most people can't work at my pace
Results-oriented	achieve results but at a cost	get the job done
Open	am sufficiently open	am not comfortable being open

Now that you have completed Columns I, II and III, it's time to compare and contrast them. There are four variations that can occur when you compare Columns II and III:

☛ **Variation #1: What they think and what they should think is exactly the same.** (#6 Conceptual) If what you are delivering and what people perceive is a positive thing, congratulations. If the statements are negative, you will have to decide what this means to you.

☛ **Variation #2: What they think and what they should think are basically the same but the language is a little different.** (#3 Personable, #8 Collaborative) Again, you will determine how or whether the similarity is meaningful to you.

☛ **Variation #3: What they think is more positive than what they should think.** (#1 Confident, #5 Self-aware, #10 Open) If you have items where the perception of you is more positive than the reality, please don't call a meeting or send out an e-mail to set the record straight. If people think more positively of you than they should, leave it alone.

☛ **Variation # 4: What they think is not as positive as what they should think.** (#4 Sensitive, #7 Influential) This is really the heart of the exercise. If what people think of you is not as positive as it should be, it is because you are not delivering the real you. You can increase your effectiveness by developing actions and strategies to help you to deliver the desired behavior to the "outside world." These actions will be dealt with in the Action Plan at the end of the chapter.

Success Step

Success Step 8.3

COLUMN I Feedback Items	COLUMN II "I think they think I..."	COLUMN III "They should think I..."	COLUMN IV "I want to be perceived as..."
Confident	am extremely confident	often doubt myself	Extremely confident
Approachable	am approachable	am a very shy person	Very approachable
Personable	am personable	like people	Personable
Sensitive	am more sensitive than I used to be	am very sensitive	A sensitive person
Self-aware	am self-aware	have to work at this	Aware of my impact on others
Conceptual	am very conceptual	am a very conceptual thinker	A conceptual thinker
Influential	am very influential	am extremely influential	A person of great influence
Collaborative	could work this a bit more	find this difficult because most people can't work at my pace	Willing to collaborate with others
Results-oriented	achieve results but at a cost	get the job done	One who knows how to execute
Open	am sufficiently open	am not comfortable being open	An open person

You may be questioning the accuracy of what others think of you. After all, you *are* just guessing. Well, you can test it by making a copy of Column II, passing it out to people in your office, and asking them to put an "X" next to anything they *disagree* with. You will probably see very few "X's." Conservatively speaking, eighty percent of What You Think They Think will be correct. You see, at some conscious or unconscious level we *do* know what people think of us. When we're forced to write it down like this, we can come up with a very clear picture.

Version II: *Specific image*

This exercise is a bit more complex because it *must* be completed over several sittings if the information is to be accurate.

Review **Success Step 8.3** on the previous page. You'll notice that you now have four columns. At the top of the page you're going to choose an individual. Jot down the name of your boss, a colleague, a customer, or a peer. This exercise is best done with at least four to six people. Plan to work on one individual per sitting. Focus only on what that individual thinks of you.

Column I: Feedback Items
Choose seven to fifteen items for each individual. You need not choose the same fifteen items for each individual but maintain a common core of at least seven items.

Column II: What Person X Thinks of Me
Write what you think that individual thinks of you.

Column III: What Person X Should Think of Me If They Knew the Real Me
Complete this just as you did in Version I.

Column IV: What Will Person X Think of Me in the Future
Write how you would like to be perceived in the future.

Interpretation

- ☛ Review the differences between Column II and Column III just as you did in Version I. Highlight the areas where Person X does not think of you as positively as he should.

- ☛ Consider the differences between Column III and Column IV. If there are differences in the way you currently are and how you want to be perceived in the future, highlight those items for action planning.

- ☛ Spread out all the sheets and review the core items. If you've done a good job of being specific, you will see how differently you behave with each person by the different way you've described the core items.

- ☛ Think about how your behavior is different with each of those individuals. By doing so, you will see how, in some cases, you don't always deliver all of your strengths and talents. It depends on whom you are with.

The bottom line is this: if people do not perceive what you think they should perceive, it's probably because *you are not delivering it.* When you compare one behavior across several people you can get a sense of what you're doing differently.

A blank version of **Success Step 8.3** is available on the next page.

Success Step

Success Step 8.3

COLUMN I **Feedback Items**	COLUMN II **"I think they think I..."**	COLUMN III **"They should think I..."**	COLUMN IV **"I want to be perceived as..."**

Success Step 8.4 | Action Plan

Action Plan

Identify the areas requiring development from the exercises discussed in this chapter. For each item, identify 2–3 specific actions you could take to be perceived as a more effective person in that area.

Item: ______________________________

Specific Actions: ______________________________

____

____

Item: ______________________________

Specific Actions: ______________________________

____

____

Item: ______________________________

Specific Actions: ______________________________

____

____

Item: ______________________________

Specific Actions: ______________________________

____

____

CHAPTER 9
Work-Life Balance

During the course of my many years of coaching, I have worked with countless workaholics. They make enormous sacrifices to accomplish their goals related to career and success, leaving wives, ex-wives, children, family, and friends in the wake. Having amassed tremendous amounts of wealth, status, and recognition, these folks often come to realize that despite their great success, their lives are empty and unfulfilled. Allow me to share a few examples with you:

I knew a woman who spent years focusing on her career and delayed having children until very late in life. Sadly, it was too late and she was unable to conceive.

There was an executive who commuted four hours a day so that his family could enjoy a big house, expensive vacations, and various enrichment activities. One day he decided to talk with them about it and learned they cared more about having him home than having things.

A young man I knew worked hard, managed his money, and retired at age 54. He was very wealthy but had never married and had no family. He was filled with regret.

There was an entrepreneur who worked extremely hard, retired at age 72, and died six months later. She left a large inheritance for her adult daughter, who lost it shortly after her mother's death. The entrepreneur's hard work was all for naught.

These tragic stories are all too common. I'm sure you know similar sad tales about workaholics. But why is it so difficult for people to balance work and life? No one ever reads the resume of the dearly departed at a funeral. Nor is the name of their workplace or organizational title on their tombstone. In the end, what we care most about is how we felt about our partner, friend, parent, or colleague. What we care most about is the quality of our relationships.

Why is everyone working so hard?

The climate in today's workplace is quite a bit different from what it was a mere thirty years ago. Back then people joined a company or organization for lifetime security. Today the expectation is that you work for a number of companies over the course of your career. And, given the insecurity that exists in today's workplace, many people feel the need to work long hours in order to demonstrate their loyalty and capabilities, and to secure a competitive advantage over their peers.

Money is another obvious answer. We all have needs and wants, and we require money to accomplish our dreams. But folks who are out of balance are often working for money, title, and position as a measure of their self-esteem and success. They are motivated less by money and more by the prestige and recognition that certain positions provide. As a result, their lives are consumed with work and they pay the hefty price of lost relationships and unfulfilled lives.

Some people have an inner drive to be at the center of everything. Others fear that the workplace will fall apart without them. So what's the answer? You've heard it before. Focus on what's important to you in life and live your life to the fullest today. But what does that really mean and how do we apply it on a daily basis? Let's first understand what Work-Life Balance is.

What is Work-Life Balance and how do we achieve it?

Work-Life Balance is the ability to manage the diverse and conflicting demands on our lives in a way that prevents one area from dominating or diminishing another.

Work-Life Balance is like a seesaw. Do you remember playing on the seesaw when you were a kid? Two people straddle a plank that is secured on a fulcrum. One goes up while the other goes down. The person whose side of the plank is down and touching the ground pushes up with his feet. Then he goes up and the other person comes down. I remember it being a lot of fun. Sometimes you could come to a point on the seesaw that allowed you and your partner to find a place of perfect balance where the two of you were suspended equally above the ground.

Often we mistakenly think that Work-Life Balance should be like the state of equilibrium on a seesaw, where everything is in equal balance. Yet, for most of us that is just not possible. Nor is it desirable. When we used to ride the seesaw it was the ups and downs that were the most fun. Sitting suspended in mid-air was a cool thing to do, but no one rides the seesaw to find a spot and remain stagnant. The real excitement was pushing up and floating down. Just like the seesaw, life's ups and downs are often scary and exciting.

As a kid, you may have run into problems on the seesaw if your partner was much heavier than you were. You probably found yourself stuck up in the air unable to come down. Or, if your partner suddenly got off the seesaw, you were sent crashing to the ground. The same can easily happen to us in life if we're managing weighty burdens. We can't quite get our feet on the ground and we miss out on the exhilaration and joy of the up and down process. Unexpected jolts in life can send us crashing to the ground, e.g., the loss of a job, an illness or death of a loved one.

By working to ensure that one area of our lives doesn't dominate or diminish another area, we can balance the ups and downs and mitigate the mid-air suspensions and sudden crashes to the ground. They're bound to happen, but just like when you were a kid, you can pick yourself up and *move on.*

How effective are you at balancing your life?

Let's take a look at the Work-Life Balance Checklist. **(Success Step 9.1)** Answer the questions honestly and score your responses.

Success Step

Success Step 9.1 | Work-Life Balance Checklist

	TRUE	FALSE
I have a priority of values that includes God, family, and work.	☐	☐
My work is not the most important thing in my life.	☐	☐
I take *all* my vacation time every year.	☐	☐
I'm there for family birthdays, games, and special events.	☐	☐
I make time for spiritual nourishment.	☐	☐
As a leader, I model appropriate work-life balance.	☐	☐
I live on a budget and within my means.	☐	☐
I exercise regularly.	☐	☐
I am not on a first-name basis with the cleaning staff.	☐	☐
I have established goals in my work and personal life.	☐	☐

Score | Give yourself 10 points for each True answer.

- ☛ *If you've scored* **90 – 100%**, *congratulations. You work hard at balancing your life.*
- ☛ *If you've scored* **80 – 89%**, *not bad. Where might you bring greater balance to your life?*
- ☛ *If you've scored* **70 – 79%**, *I suspect your family and/or co-workers would like to see you make some changes.*
- ☛ *If you've scored* **below 70%**, *continue reading.*

What are some specific things you can do to manage your life and your work?

Define success in a way that is both meaningful to you and satisfies your values. You have to decide if rising to the top is workable and desirable for you. Can you manage the demands of such a challenging career choice and still get home to play baseball with your son, attend your daughter's soccer games, play a round of hoops with friends, or take a yoga class? If so, go for it! If you think you'll have to make sacrifices that are too big to manage, reconsider.

Talk to your family. Many people make the erroneous assumption that they're doing what's right for the family by working long hours to make money and get ahead. A mother of two young adults once shared with me that she had made the choice to put work first. Now she regrets having made that choice, given the enormous price her family had to pay. Do you know how kids spell love? T-I-M-E. They want mommy and daddy at home. And so do your partners. Talk to your family. Make sure that your goals are in sync with what the family desires.

Protect the relationships that are important to you. How do you protect the relationships that are important to you *and* balance the demands of work and family? You have to choose what's important to you and then make these things top priority. Develop some policies by which you will live. For example, you need to decide how much sleep you need and when will be the best time to exercise. Many people work from home one or two days per week. On a monthly basis, how many weekends might you spend with friends or family or just stay home to pamper yourself? Schedule your yearly vacations and then plan your work around them. Watch for signs of burnout or imbalance such as poor eating habits, ineffectiveness at work, or spending an inordinate amount of time vegging out in front of the television. Determine how many times you will work late during the week or how many days will you be out of town on a business trip, or how often you will schedule massages, have your nails done, or spend time alone.

Evaluate your priorities regularly. If you are an achiever, and it's likely that you are since you are reading this book, you probably get a lot of invitations to get involved in different organizations, charities, volunteer associations, and the like. And, because we live in a society replete with overstimulation, opportunities and activities can creep up and slip into our day-to-day lives without our being aware. Before we know it, we're hopelessly overcommitted. I suggest that you reevaluate your activities and commitments at least once or twice a year. Then ask yourself whether these activities and commitments are consistent with your values and definition of success.

Work in an environment that supports your values. *Recently I had a client, Bill, who was on the fast track, but his workplace environment was extraordinarily demanding. Working on Saturdays was commonplace for Bill because there was just so much to do. He'd arrive at work early in the morning and stay until very late in the evening. This simply was not a good fit for Bill since he had a young family and a very unhappy wife. When an opportunity became available, Bill opted to move to another location within his company. The new position was not as visible as his previous one, but Bill had found a situation that better complimented his family's needs and goals. When I asked him about his decision to take himself off the fast track, he told me that the new position is just as challenging as the previous one, but that it doesn't require the long hours. The biggest plus for Bill is that his organization still considers him a "high caliber performer."* Consider Bill's "before and after" statistics:

	Before	After
Blood Pressure	135/80	100/79
Weekday Dinner With Family	0–1 per week	3–5 per week
Miles Run	0–3 per week	6–12 per week
Hours Worked Per Week	60++	50+
Weekends Worked	2 per month	0–1 per month
Marriage	Wife very concerned	She tells him he's like a new person

Learn to say "no." This is difficult for many people. But saying "yes" all the time does not allow other people, who could and should say yes, to grow and develop their skills. More importantly, you become overworked and unable to meet your own needs and the needs of your family. You place the order, but they pay the bill.

Set goals, schedule time. It is important to have daily, weekly, and monthly goals so that you are clear on what you need to accomplish on a day-to-day basis. But you also need to schedule the activities required to accomplish those goals. The discipline of scheduling your activities develops your judgment about what you can realistically accomplish in a given time frame. A realistic assessment of your capabilities reduces stress. Scheduling causes you to focus on getting out of the office on time, getting to the gym, making it to your children's events, or meeting friends for dinner. You learn how to *not* waste time. The people that I know who have really good Work-Life Balance are extraordinarily goal-oriented. It's not that they can't have casual conversations at work, but they're very, very conscious of trying to maximize their time at work so that they can be with family and friends at a reasonable hour. They tend to take shorter lunches, they don't procrastinate, and they manage the distractions that threaten to take them away from their tasks.

Manage only one calendar. It doesn't matter if it's a Blackberry, a Palm Pilot, or a Franklin planner — choose one and stick with it. You need to begin to see your life as whole. Managing separate calendars for work, your personal life, and your children's events will have you overscheduled and overwhelmed.

Keep things simple. I'm sure that you've all sat in meetings and thought, "Why are we spending so much time on this one item?" In the workplace, we can overcomplicate things, and we end up wasting lots of time as a result. My rule is: The simpler the better. People are much more impressed when they "get" what you're trying to say than they are by your use of complicated jargon or highly technical information. But don't make the mistake of underestimating your colleagues' intelligence by being unprepared at meetings. When you do, you waste their time and you create undue stress and frustration.

Live within your means. Overspending will have you working overtime to pay off the bills you've amassed. While you may have lots of new things, the downside is that you end up missing out on other aspects of life. You may even find yourself taking a job that you don't really enjoy simply because it pays better, just to keep the bill collectors at bay. Debt will have you on the seesaw, stuck in midair, unable to get your feet on the ground.

Take time to play. Schedule fun time if you must. In Chapter 4, we talked about the importance of having a healthy, Free Child. So plan to spend time with your partner, friends, or kids. Get out for dinner, go to a concert, do something that gets you to laugh.

Have other interests in your life besides work. Meeting new people who have different experiences and perspectives can sometimes help us see life differently. In the workplace, those at the top represent success to us. When we work with others who are not as privileged as we are, we can see how successful we truly are. Consider taking a volunteer role in your local school system, your church or synagogue, or within your community.

Get organized. One of my clients was planning to relocate because her apartment was so disorganized and full of so much clutter that the only way she could eliminate the problem was to move. She had a great apartment in New York City. I suggested that she not move or attempt to organize the apartment on her own. I recommended that she hire Marva Ruot, a professional organizer. They spent two days together, and as a result, my client is now living a more organized and stress-free life. According to Marva, "visual clutter in the home or workplace is psychologically debilitating and physically exhausting. It encourages procrastination, causes confusion, reduces productivity, stifles creativity and is depressing." Get help if you need it. It's been estimated that we spend approximately two weeks each year trying to find things. Becoming more organized can return that extra two weeks to you to work, rest, or play.

Take time to "Do You." Why is it that when something comes up at work requiring more of our time, we are somehow able to squeeze it in? But when it comes to having time for ourselves, we just can't seem to find the time. I block certain non-vacation weeks and days on my calendar so that I can have what I call "down time." If you call my office and attempt to schedule a meeting on those dates, you will be told, "she's booked." And I am...with myself. How do we take time for ourselves? You have to see yourself as a priority item to be placed on the calendar. Notice that I didn't use the term "find" time for yourself, as if time were hidden somewhere under a rock. You must begin to set boundaries around time you commit to use for yourself. This is the only way that you can realistically get to the gym, take a walk, read, put your feet up, catch the game or a great movie on TV, go to the park, or just plain relax. You've got to *make* time. You're not going to find it. Certainly you've heard the metaphor about the rock and the bowl which says: if we had a bowl, a pitcher of water, some rocks, and some sand, and we decided to put all of this into the bowl, these items would probably not all fit if we put the sand in first, then the water, and then the rocks. But if we put the rocks in first, then the sand, and then the water, they would all fit. Similarly, in our lives we have to schedule the most important things first, i.e., family, friends, and ourselves. The others will fit in, but not until the biggest items are in first.

Stay in shape. It's important to stay as healthy as you can. See your doctor regularly, and don't ignore obvious changes in your health. As you're getting older, make a habit of getting to the gym regularly and eating a healthy diet. Good health and a fit body will protect against disease and cause you to have a vibrant and more satisfying life.

It is said that good trees bring forth good fruit. I believe that truly successful people leave a fruitful legacy of strong family relationships, good friends, respect, and admiration. No one ever lays on their deathbed wishing they had spent more time at work. Balancing work and life is the only way to accomplish a life well spent.

Success Step 9.2 | Work-Life Balance Action Plan

Action Plan

Review your responses on the Work-Life Balance Checklist and determine three actions you would like to take to bring balance to your life.

1. ______________________________

____

____

2. ______________________________

____

____

3. ______________________________

____

____

CHAPTER 10

Crossing the Finish Line

If you have read all the preceding chapters, you have completed a pretty extensive process of self-assessment and discovery. As gratifying as this may be, to stop now would be like Dorothy, the Tin Man, the Lion, and the Scarecrow stopping at the gates of Emerald City without asking the Wizard of Oz what they came for — a trip back to Kansas, a heart, courage, and a brain.

You may recall that before the Wizard would grant their wishes, they first had to defeat the Wicked Witch of the West. Similarly, before you can go on to enjoy a more successful life you will need to do one last thing: say goodbye to old behaviors and develop a strategy for a more "Successful You."

Real life is neither fantasy or fairy tale. You're not going to wake up, discover your difficulties were only a bad dream, and enjoy a happy ending. You can only increase your personal and professional influence by working on it. You need a plan — wishing won't make it so.

Our objective in this chapter is to review the information that has been generated in the previous chapters, identify your key developmental opportunities, and develop the Ready, Set, Grow! Action Plan to help you grow and stay on track.

Let's look back

Begin by reviewing your completed worksheets. Get them out in front of you and take a good look. You should be feeling pretty good about your accomplishments and you probably have a greater sense of who you are and what's important to you. Your personal Vision of Success (Chapter 3) is now in focus.

To develop a strategy that takes you from today's reality to your Vision of Success, we're going to do some final exercises, starting with the Force Field Analysis — **Illustration 10.1** below.

Illustration

Illustration 10.1 | Force Field Analysis

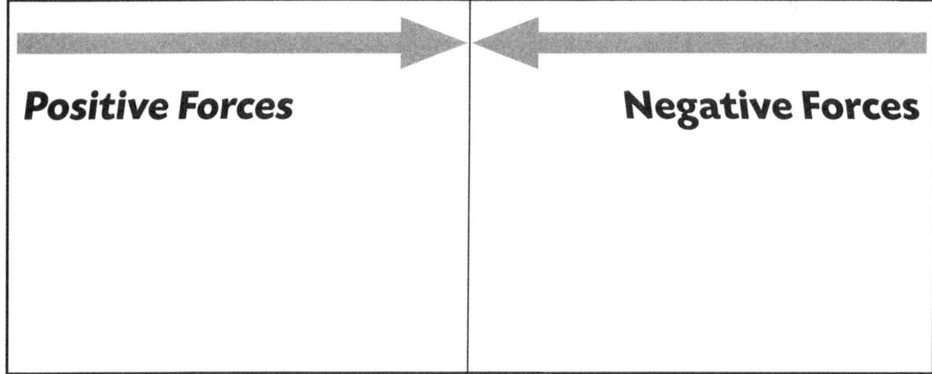

Kurt Lewin, a pioneer in the social sciences, developed this model back the 1940s. Lewin believed that in any situation there are both driving and restraining forces that influence our ability to change. He postulated that where we are today regarding any situation is a balance between negative and positive forces. Further, when negative and positive forces meet and establish a state of equilibrium, our Current State is established.

Consider your weight as an example. Hopefully, you have good things working for you like a healthy diet and exercise, but you may also have a few things working against you such as your age, an illness, or your love of chocolate. If you eat a low fat diet but fail to exercise, negative forces may be too much of an obstacle for your healthy diet to overcome. If this occurs, excess poundage will likely result.

When I work with the Force Field Analysis, I like to start with the Desired State. **(Illustration 10.2)**

Illustration 10.2 | Force Field Analysis: Desired State

Illustration

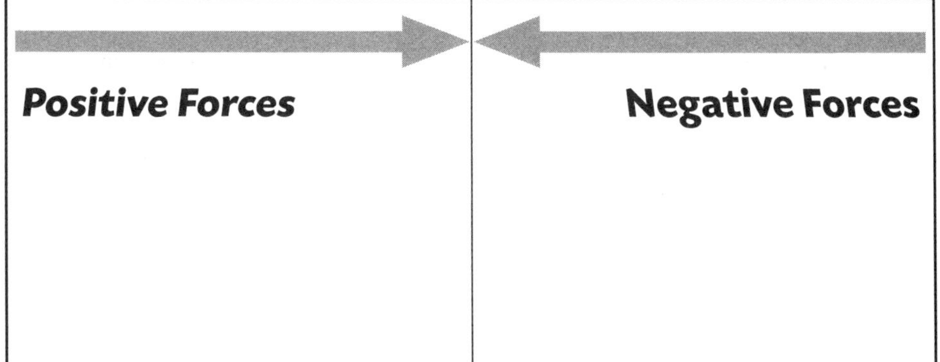

Review your Vision of Success and do your best to briefly state where you see yourself in the future (Desired State). On **Illustration 10.2** write your Desired State. A fully fleshed-out vision would require several paragraphs, but for the purposes of this exercise a three- or-four word description will do.

Look at the section titled Worst Case Scenario. If you did nothing and started to slide backwards, what would your worst possible scenario look like? Write that down.

Having recorded your Worst Case Scenario, take a few minutes now to write a summary statement describing your Current State, or where you are today.

Consider what you've written in your Current State summary, and think about your Desired State. Jot down the positive forces that are pushing you toward your Desired State under the arrow to the left of the Current State. (See **Illustration 10.3** on the following page for an example.)

Illustration

Illustration 10.3 | Force Field Analysis: The Positive & Negative Forces

Unemployed	**Manager**	**Senior Vice President**
Worst Case Scenario	**Current Status**	**Desired State**

Positive Forces →	← **Negative Forces**
☛ *Committed to succeed*	☛ *Competitive environment*
☛ *Pursuing advanced degree*	☛ *Limited opportunities*
☛ *Having good success in current position*	☛ *No mentor*
☛ *Well liked*	

You probably have many positive things going for you. It is imperative that you get them down on paper in order to carefully consider them. For example, as a result of all the work that you've done in this book, you may have learned that you have excellent communication skills or that you relate to people well, or even that you really know your business, etc. These are all positive forces that help move you toward your Desired State. If there were no opposing or negative forces (things that work against you), the line that represents your Current State would easily move toward the Desired State without incident. But the reality is that there are usually forces working against you. Let's identify what they are.

As you think about what it takes to achieve your Desired State, brainstorm the opposing forces (things that work against you). On **Illustration 10.3**, write them under the arrow to the right of the Current State. Thankfully, you have positive forces to counteract the opposing forces. Otherwise they would push you toward that worst-case scenario without resistance.

Before you can focus on the critical forces that work both for and against you, you must identify the strength of these forces.

Let's keep this simple. On a scale of 1 to 5 (1 being low and 5 being high), decide the strength or intensity of each force. You can represent that by drawing an arrow of the length that represents the numerical strength under each force (See **Illustration 10.4**). Do this for both the positive and opposing forces. Using different colored pens will make it easier to visualize.

Now that you've identified the strength of each force, let's evaluate what you have.

Illustration

**Illustration 10.4 | Force Field Analysis:
Identifying the Strength of Positive & Negative Forces**

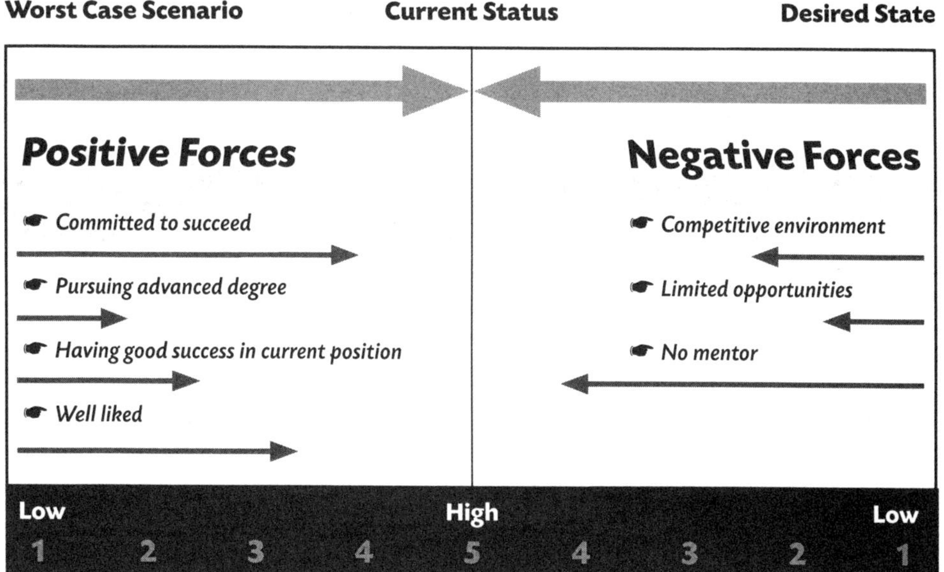

As you look at the positive forces that move you toward your Desired State, identify the weaker forces (1s & 2s). Highlight them by putting a circle around them. (See **Illustration 10.5** on the next page.)

Illustration

Illustration 10.5 | Force Field Analysis: Identifying the Strength of Positive & Negative Forces

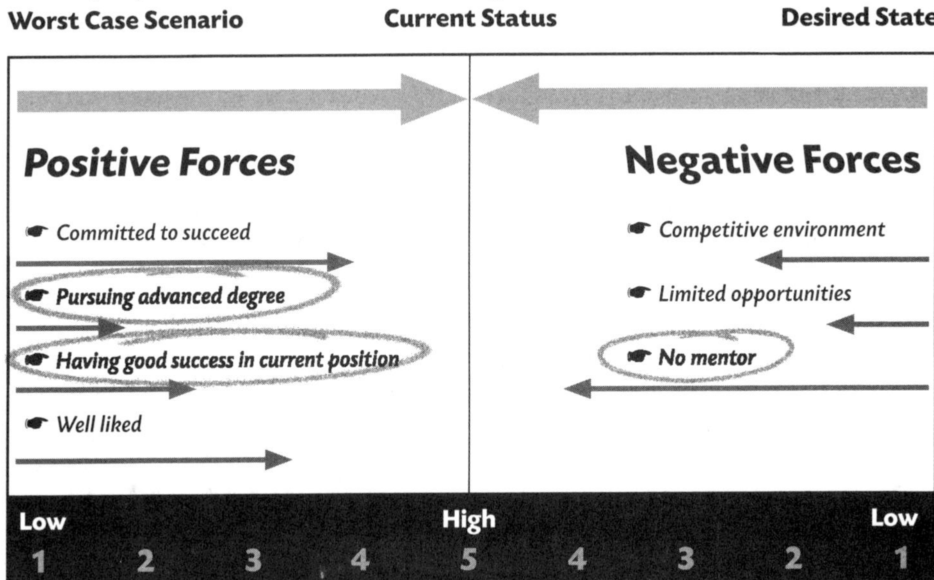

The objective in highlighting these weaker positive forces is to strengthen them so that they give you greater impetus to move toward your Desired State.

On the opposing side, identify and circle the stronger forces (4s & 5s). The objective here is to reduce their strength and weaken the forces that cause resistance.

You have assessed the strength of each force and identified the specific issues that will require special attention. You will now need to develop two or three actions to strengthen a positive force or lessen an opposing one. (See **Success Step 10.1**)

Review the actions after you have written them. If you read an action and find yourself asking, "*How* am I going to accomplish this?", the action must be more specific so that it promotes action.

Success Step 10.1 | Action Items

Action Plan

Developmental Opportunities (positive forces to be strengthened or negative forces to be weakened)

____

____

Actions: ______________________________

____

Developmental Opportunities (positive forces to be strengthened or negative forces to be weakened)

____

____

Actions: ______________________________

____

Developmental Opportunities (positive forces to be strengthened or negative forces to be weakened)

____

____

Actions: ______________________________

____

Suppose, for example, I decided to focus on my weak communication skills. I could write the following actions: I'm going to be more present in meetings, I'm going to be more visible, and I'm going to communicate better. These actions sound good, but they are not specific enough. I need to ask myself *how* am I going to be more present in meetings, *how* am I going to become more visible, and *how* will I become a better communicator? A specific action would be: I'm going to ask at least three questions at every meeting I attend, I'm going to ask my boss if I can present the departmental results at the quarterly meeting, and I'm going to register for the next Presentation Skills class at the Adult School. You must be able to specifically *see* the action. (See **Illustration 10.6**)

Illustration

Illustration 10.6 | How to Fill Out Success Step 10.1 Worksheet

Developmental Opportunities (positive forces to be strengthened or negative forces to be weakened)

I am a weak communicator.

Actions: I'm going to ask at least three questions at every meeting I attend.

I'm going to ask my boss if I can present the departmental results at the quarterly meeting.

I'm going to register for the next Presentation Skills class at the Adult School.

Ask a friend or colleague to review your actions to be sure that the actions you choose are specific. Writing solidly specific actions will almost guarantee your success.

Now that you've decided on the appropriate actions, you'll need to plug them into your Success Strategies Action Plan. **(Success Step 10.2)** Once you've written all your actions in the appropriate spaces, identify the obstacles that could prevent you from achieving them. Include time frames so that you have a specific deadline to reference for achieving them. And identify an accountability partner — someone you can e-mail, call, or meet with to discuss your progress on a regular basis. This is critical! Maintaining an accountability relationship will keep you honest about your progress.

Success Step 10.2 | Ready, Set, Grow! Action Plan

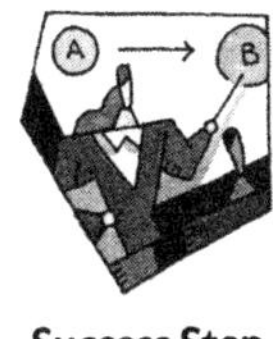

Success Step

Actions	Obstacles	Time Frame	Accountability Partner

Your Ready, Set, Grow! Action Plan may be very lengthy or it may be relatively short. If it *is* lengthy, it will be difficult to keep it at a conscious level on a daily basis. I suggest that you review the entire list and apply Pareto's Law, better known as the 80-20 Rule. The 80-20 Rule suggests that we can expect 80 percent of our results from 20 percent of our resources or effort. For example, 20 percent of an organization's sales force will generate 80 percent of the sales. Eighty percent of the people problems that managers deal with in the workplace come from 20 percent of the staff. Twenty percent of the space in your home generates 80 percent of the dust or clutter.

The 80/20 Rule

80% of your success is determined by 20% of your effort

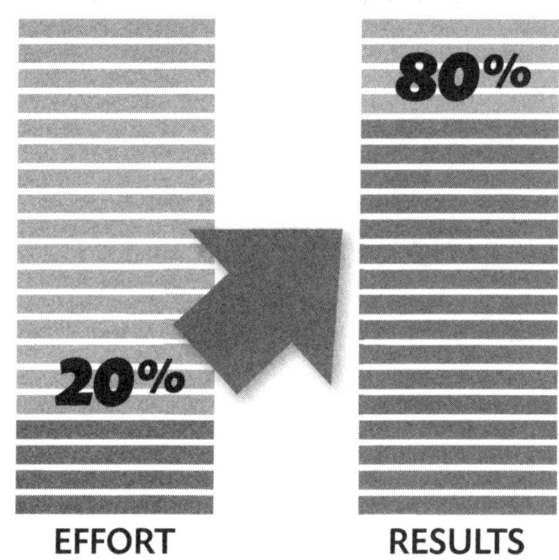

When you look at your list of Strategic Actions, you can expect to achieve 80 percent of your impact from 20 percent of those items. Determine which of these actions are the "Critical Few," or those that will give you the greatest impact. Write them on **Success Step 10.3**. You can carry these power-packed actions with you and perform a check on how you're doing on a daily or weekly basis. The Ready, Set, Grow! Action Plan should be reviewed monthly or quarterly at the very least. But the Power Pack Checklist is the one that will really keep you on track because you will review it more frequently.

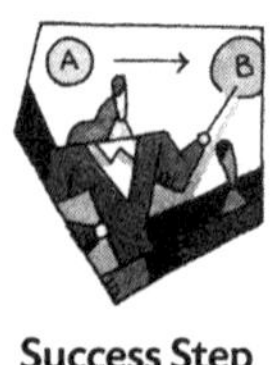

Success Step

Success Step 10.3 | Power Pack Checklist — The Critical Few

	ON TARGET	NOT ON TARGET
Count to ten when I feel self becoming too aggressive	☐	☐
Allow others to complete their thoughts before speaking	☐	☐
Walk the floor and connect with staff	☐	☐

Success Step 10.3 | Power Pack Checklist — Action Plan

	ON TARGET	NOT ON TARGET
	☐	☐
	☐	☐
	☐	☐
	☐	☐
	☐	☐
	☐	☐
	☐	☐
	☐	☐

Be sure you discuss with your accountability partner how often you would like to review the Ready, Set, Grow! Action Plan. Schedule time and follow through. Revisit the goals you wrote in Chapter 1. Attach this plan and keep them together.

Congratulations! You've made it to the Finish Line. You are obviously very serious about your growth and development. People who accomplish this level of effort are highly successful. This type of dedication and determination will continue to strengthen your confidence and increase your ability to succeed. It's in your hands now. Good Work!

About Your Coach

I doubt any of my friends from high school or college would be surprised to learn that I grew up to be a Leadership Development Strategist and Coach. After all, I was a senior class officer, a student government officer in high school, and in college I served in various positions of influence and authority. Perhaps the person who is most surprised, though, is me.

When I graduated from college with a B.S. degree in Special Education, I believed I was destined for a career working with special needs children. In fact, I did enjoy teaching for a few years in the Virgin Islands. But I wanted to live closer to my family in Connecticut so fate brought me to New York and the opposite end the continuum, i.e., working with gifted and talented adults.

Learning how to coach was very difficult. In fact, those first few years were very difficult. In those early days, there were no training programs, certifications or coaching associations. The work was challenging and there were times when I wanted to quit. If anyone had told me then that I would still be coaching more than 20 years later, I would not have believed it. But I grew into the role and the role grew on me.

Here is my story:
My work in Leadership Development began in 1974. While employed by a major New York City financial services organization, I was responsible for designing and conducting professional and leadership development programs for supervisors

and first level managers. I enjoyed my work as a Director of Training for a 4000-member division. I was an internal consultant and loved the diversity of projects and people with whom I worked. When I decided to start my own business, I wrote a one-page business plan and went for professional counseling. I was told not to quit my day job, stay the corporate route for a while, and get a little more seasoning and a few more promotions. It was good advice and I followed it.

In 1982, I joined a small consulting firm called Donchian Management Services, which was founded by Dikran Donchian, a true pioneer in the field of Executive Coaching. Back in the 70s, women and minorities had begun entering corporate environs in significant numbers. Dik observed that these populations did not do as well as their white, male counterparts. They were certainly as intelligent and well educated, but stylistically they didn't manage themselves as well. He designed a six-month Individual Executive Development Program to address the softer skills of style, leadership, relationships, managing one's self and others: virtually everything that fell outside the technical or functional aspects of one's job. We worked with each individual client as a team of two, an older white male and a younger black female. It was a powerful model to have someone older, younger, male, female, and black and white sitting at the table.

Coaching only began to come into its own as a discipline in the 1990s, so in the early 80s it was difficult to describe what we did. We positioned ourselves as pragmatic business people, as opposed to social workers or psychologists. We did not want people to be fearful that there might be something wrong with them if they thought we were some type of counselor.

We drew a distinction between training and development, which many people thought of as one and the same thing. We defined training as any activity that enhanced a functional or technical skill such as public speaking or learning a particular type of software. Development was any activity that enhanced the softer skills I've described above. Training had a particular set of objectives and could usually be accomplished in a short period of time. Development could only be accomplished over an extended period of time because of the discovery process required to uncover the real issues that hurt or help performance in the workplace.

The work was meaningful but, as I said earlier, difficult. Frankly, I did not enjoy it then as much as I do today. I had to find my own voice and that took a few years. But the foundation that was laid as a result of working with DMS was invaluable. Dik died in 1984. I worked for his widow, Karen, for the next six months to complete the unfinished work, and then started my own consulting practice in

1985. I believe Dik would be as pleased with me now as I am of having had him as a boss and a mentor.

Today, I stand proudly on my 20 years of experience, wisdom and expertise in developing leaders. I have seen so many people grow in their careers and achieve the highest levels of accomplishment in their organizations. I am equally proud of those who, through our process of self-discovery, have identified who they are as an authentic and integrated person.

I did not write this book to talk about coaching. Rather, it is meant to be a coaching tool. The Success Strategies put forth here represent the issues that are most common to the many hundreds of leaders with whom I have worked. It is my belief that these Success Strategies can help you more effectively manage the vicissitudes of work life and lead you to becoming a more successful person.

Scripture tells us: "To every thing there is a season, and a time to every purpose under the heaven" (Ecclesiastes 3:1).

Now is the time to move into your season and your purpose. I encourage you to get *Ready, Set, Grow!*

VJ Holcomb Associates

Transforming Challenge to Opportunity®

Leadership Development Coaching Programs

Established in New York in 1985, VJ Holcomb Associates is dedicated to supporting leaders who seek to serve their organizations at their highest level of influence and impact. We guide top company leaders and teams to achieve greater levels of professional effectiveness and organizational success through customized leadership development coaching and training that provides guidance, affirmation and accountability.

Individual Executive Development Program

12-month process of assessment, analysis, coaching, action planning and follow-on

Power Coaching

Short-term and focused skill development and/or behavior modification

Customized Leadership Development Programs

Extended workshop training and individual coaching — ideal for teams or affinity groups that need support in reaching the next level

Follow-On Coaching

For participants who have completed the Individual Executive Development or Power Coaching Program — provides refinement, accountability and an ongoing sounding board

Resources for Professional Trainers and Leadership Coaches

VJ Holcomb Associates is a resource for online professional self-discovery and development programs. We serve individuals, in-house corporate trainers and other organizational development consultants. We provide validated, reliable and award-winning training and assessment products for traditional instructor-led formats as well as computer and web-based learning.

Ready, Set, Grow! Facilitation System

The Ready,Set,Grow! Facilitation System is a powerful tool for professional growth and development. Based on the book, *Ready, Set,*

Grow! 10 Success Strategies for Winning in the Workplace, this system contains a comprehensive curriculum designed to engage the learner through experiential group and individual activities. The convenient and flexible modular design includes detailed lesson plans and objectives and affords trainers and facilitators the opportunity to create learning solutions of any length. Integrated technology includes PowerPoint slides to enhance training, lecturettes, and training vignettes using DVD and CD-ROM technology.

Coach-the-Coach

This program teaches our proven methodology and insights for successful one-on-one coaching. The methodology employs a careful process of analysis, reinforcement of existing strengths, and identification of actions and strategies for increased effectiveness.

Internal Coach-the-Coach Program

This program provides organizations the opportunity to train and equip a cadre of internal coaches with the skills and benefits of one-on-one coaching. By using a consistent methodology and personnel who have first-hand insight into the organization, an internal coaching program can support corporate strategy for developing interpersonal competence and leadership effectiveness.

Assessment Instruments

We offer high quality, easy-to-use learning instruments for individual, team, and organizational success. Assessments are available for training in Communications, Conflict Management, Team Innovation, Time Management, Mentoring, Self-Management, Leading Others, and Coaching. Most assessments can be completed online, and Facilitator Kits are available for all topics as well as for several self-contained programs.

Train-the-Trainer

VJ Holcomb Associates' professional staff can train your personnel to work with our instruments and resources in order to implement in-house programs.

Detailed information on all our programs and resources is available at **www.vjholcomb.com.**

Index

G

H

I

J

K

L

M

N

O

P

R

S

T

U

V

W

X